MW00993946

THE GOOD, THE BAD, AND THE UGLY
OAKLAND RAIDERS

THE GOOD, THE BAD, AND THE UGLY OAKLAND RAIDERS

HEART-POUNDING, JAW-DROPPING, AND GUT-WRENCHING MOMENTS IN OAKLAND RAIDERS HISTORY

Steven Travers

TRIUMPH
BOOKS

Library of Congress Cataloging-in-Publication Data

Travers, Steven.
The good, the bad, and the ugly Oakland Raiders : heart-pounding, jaw-dropping, and gut-wrenching moments from Oakland Raiders history / Steven Travers.
p. cm.
ISBN-13: 978-1-57243-927-6
ISBN-10: 1-57243-927-0
1. Oakland Raiders (Football team)—History. 2. Football players—United States—Anecdotes. I. Title.

GV956.O24T73 2008
796.332'640979494—dc22

2008005823

This book is available in quantity at special discounts for your group or organization. For further information, contact:

Triumph Books
542 South Dearborn Street
Suite 750
Chicago, Illinois 60605
(312) 939-3330
Fax (312) 663-3557

Printed in U.S.A.
ISBN-13: 978-1-57243-927-6
Design by Patricia Frey.
Editorial production by Prologue Publishing Services, LLC.
All photos courtesy of Ron Riesterer unless otherwise indicated.

To Mom,
who raised a sports fanatic but balanced that with culture, thus creating a well-rounded man.
Thanks for puttin' up with me.

CONTENTS

Foreword by Bruce Macgowan ix

Acknowledgments xvi

Introduction xvii

Stadium Stories 1
- The San Francisco Raiders? 1
- Daddy Dearest: Al Davis and the Ownership Group 5

The Good 11
- Football's Napoleon 11
- "The Mad Bomber" 14
- Double Zero 19
- The Promised Land 23
- "Guys Do Stuff" 29
- "The Greatness That Is the Raiders" 33
- Kings of Tinsel Town 38

The Bad 43
- Merger 43
- So Close, and Yet So Far 47
- No Repeat in '77 52

The Ugly 59
- "The Immaculate Reception" 59

Hunter Thompson, the Hell's Angels, and the Criminal Element 66
The Assassin 72

In the Clutch 77
1963–1965: Saving the Oakland Franchise 77
The Miracle Worker 82
"The Sea of Hands" 88
"Home of Champions" 94
Snake 99
The Best Slow Hall of Fame Receiver Money Can Buy 104

It Ain't Over 'Til It's Over 108
Commitment to Excellence 108
The Heidi Game 113
Knockin' on the Door of Greatness 119
"Just Win, Baby!" 123
Amazing Grace 128
Rich Gannon and the 2002 Super Bowl Team 133

Winners 139
Upshaw 139
Flores and Shell 143
The Real Willie Brown 147
Golden Boy 151
Howie, Stork, Raiderettes, and the "Five-Oh" 155
Ronnie Lott 159
The King of Them All 161

A Little Intrigue 165
Football's CIA 165
The Raiders Plunder the 'Niners 169

All-Time Raiders Team 174
Defense 174
Offense 174
Special Teams 176

Trivia Answers 177

FOREWORD

Bruce Macgowan, a longtime KNBR 680 sports personality, is a friend of the author's. The two of them regaled San Francisco and Oakland press box denizens with their dead-on movie imitations from Spartacus, Three Days In May, *and other classics. Bruce is a graduate—as is Steve Travers—of Redwood High School in Marin County, where he was a classmate of USC football coach Pete Carroll. One of the most respected sports-talk hosts and reporters on either side of the Bay Area, Macgowan has covered "the greatness that is the Raiders" for more than two decades.*

* * *

I was one lucky kid. Growing up in Northern California in the 1960s was never boring. San Francisco was a magical place. I could see the lights of the city glittering off the waters of the bay at night, and foghorns played a sad and haunting lullaby as the hours wore deep into the late evening. Part of the routine in our family was to do what many people liked to do from time to time, and that was to drive across the Golden Gate Bridge to the magical city of San Francisco. My parents would put on their best clothes, and my brother and I would don blazers and ties, and we would go to dinner in North Beach, or perhaps attend a play downtown. Occasionally my dad would take us out for a special afternoon of fun at the old Playland by the Beach (which has long since disappeared), or perhaps a ballgame. Going to Candlestick Park to see Willie Mays and the Giants, or to dowdy old Kezar Stadium to watch Y.A. Tittle and the 49ers was always a special treat.

By the latter part of the decade, things had changed radically. The beatniks were starting to disappear in North Beach, and the hippies were showing up in Haight Ashbury for wild and uninhibited times that included plenty of rock and roll, drugs, and sex. It was an exciting period! There were also plenty of protests against a divisive and escalating war in Southeast Asia, as college students at Berkeley and San Francisco State tried to shut down the campuses to bring attention to the matter.

The only time I ever seemed to venture across the bridge to the East Bay was when I went with my friend and his dad (a Cal alum) to see the Golden Bears and their All-American quarterback Craig Morton play powerhouse rivals from UCLA or USC. One time I remember going to a concert performed by the Oakland Symphony, as my junior high music teacher, who played the oboe, was a featured performer.

Until the Raiders moved into small and rickety Frank Youell Field, just south of downtown Oakland, the poor city across the bay was considered a nonentity. The late, great sportswriter Wells Twombly once described Oakland as a town with "beer on its breath, a stubble on its chin, and a hard hat on its head."

Although the Raiders struggled early, things changed dramatically with the arrival of a brash, 33-year-old head coach named Al Davis, and the rest, as they say, "is history."

My first experience watching the Raiders came in the mid-1960s when my dad and I took in a game between the Raiders and the Buffalo Bills. Quarterbacks Tom Flores of Oakland and Jack Kemp of the Bills (later a key political figure in the 1980s) put on quite a show that day, and the Raiders won a typically high-scoring, freewheeling battle.

For someone who had only a passing interest in the then-mediocre 49ers, I found myself rooting hard for the Raiders and thoroughly enjoying the old American Football League.

I also remember going to the local five-and-dime store in my hometown in southern Marin and buying those distinctive, one-time-only AFL bubble gum cards of 1965, and I'm proud to say I still have the entire collection. Besides Flores, I was able to find the cards of such young stars as center Jim Otto, running back Clem Daniels, and wide receivers Art Powell and Bo Roberson in the packs that I'd buy with a quarter.

From their distinctive silver-and-black uniforms to their gradual rise to the top of the pro game, the Raiders entranced younger and older fans alike throughout the region. By the time the Raiders moved into the new Oakland Coliseum in 1966, a love affair between the team and the fans was blooming, and the working-class folks in the East Bay could finally puff out their chest proudly as if to say to the folks across the bridge, "Hey look at us!" While the media then, as today, loved to paint a caricature of Raiders fans as "part Hell's Angels, part Black Panthers," in truth, the fringe characters might have been only a small part of the scene in those perennial sell-out crowds at the Oakland Coliseum.

Two of my favorite memories from that era involve two games I attended in person. In November of 1968, the Raiders' matchup with the up-and-coming New York Jets and their flamboyant quarterback Joe Namath turned out to be a cult classic, later known as the "Heidi Game." The only seats my dad and I were able to get the week before the game were in the north end zone, and I still have the stubs, which show a $3.50 admission charge. What a game we saw that day! The score ping-ponged back and forth before the Jets appeared to put themselves in good shape on a Jim Turner field goal with just under two minutes to play. We later learned that NBC, because the game was running over its allotted time, unwisely decided to cut away from the action to show the television special *Heidi*. In those days, the games were blacked out locally, but most of the rest of the country, including the East, South, and Midwestern regions, missed the incredible finish.

With Oakland driving for what they hoped would be a game-winning touchdown or at least a tying field goal, quarterback Daryle Lamonica, who was better known as the "Mad Bomber," instead fired a short pass in the right flat to a little-known rookie running back named Charlie Smith. Smith shed one tackle, got behind a couple of defenders, and then outdistanced a Jets cornerback to race in for a go-ahead touchdown. Pandemonium erupted, but the excitement wasn't over. On the ensuing kickoff, Jets return man Earl Christy was bumped into by one of his own teammates who jarred the ball loose, and an obscure special-teams player named Preston Ridlehuber enjoyed his 15 minutes of fame by recovering the football in the end zone. Incredible! In 28 seconds, the Raiders had scored twice and turned a 32–29 deficit into a 43–32 victory.

This was the first of just many such amazing comebacks performed by what announcer Bill King later called, "the Miracle Team."

Now fast forward to 1974 for an even more amazing finish. Considered one of the game's powerhouse teams for the better part of 10 years, Oakland was hosting the two-time defending champion Miami Dolphins in a first-round playoff game on a cool, overcast December afternoon. Again my dad and I were lucky enough to buy tickets well in advance (I remember standing in line for four hours at the Raiders' old offices across the street from the Coliseum on Oakland Street in an effort to purchase them).

By 1974 many of the faces on the Oakland roster had changed, including the head coach (now John Madden) and the quarterback (now Kenny Stabler). While they had been frustrated by a lot of near misses in the postseasons of the late '60s and early '70s, Oakland fans never had to suffer through the tedium of a lost season. The Raiders won nearly 90 percent of their games in those years, and by then they had also developed a penchant for routinely pulling out last-second victories.

When 43-year-old George Blanda delivered game-winning field goals and touchdown passes during an incredible five-game streak in 1970, fans all over the country began to take notice. You might remember that 1970 was also the year when the old American Football League and the established NFL merged into one mighty league. That was also the first year of ABC's *Monday Night Football*, and the weekly game became an instant prime-time classic to millions of viewers, turning broadcasters Howard Cosell, Frank Gifford, and "Dandy Don" Meredith into pop culture icons.

The merger between the two leagues combined with the appearance of the national game of the week on prime-time television was a perfect marriage that brought the game to a level of excitement and interest never before experienced in this country.

By 1974 the Dolphins were one of the league's great stories, as they had won back-to-back Super Bowls, taking the title in 1972 with the only perfect season in league history, and then crushing the Raiders in the 1973 AFC Title game 27–10 on their way to a second straight crown. Miami head coach Don Shula, however, realized that the matchup with the Raiders might be the end of a great run for his team, as star running backs Jim Kiick and Larry Csonka and wide receiver Paul Warfield would be leaving the next season to join the fledgling World Football League.

Dolphins fans in those years of the early '70s developed a unique habit that became quite popular in South Florida. Exhorted over the radio by play-by-play announcer Rick Weaver to "wave your hankies!" Miami fans celebrated touchdowns and subsequent wins by displaying a wave of fluttering handkerchiefs throughout the Orange Bowl.

When the Dolphins jogged onto the field for the first-round playoff game against the Raiders, the Oakland fans were ready to respond in kind. Not only were Miami players rudely greeted with thunderous boos and catcalls, but the stands at the Oakland Coliseum erupted as fans waved thousands of black handkerchiefs, shirts, team jerseys, and other assorted black-colored items from the stands. I even saw a fellow a few rows over waving what looked to be a woman's black nightie, while his buddy in the seat nearby proudly circled over his head what appeared to be a pair of black panties.

John Madden later described the scene and the noise as the "most incredible and loudest I've ever seen in our place." For a full half an hour before kickoff, the noise and demonstration continued unabated. Then came the kickoff, and as Madden later described it: "You've got this crescendo of noise...*and bap!* We kick off. What happens next? Some guy named Nat Moore runs it back [89] yards for a score, and they take the lead right there in our place! In front of our fans!"

But that stunning kick return by the rookie Moore was only a prelude to an even more incredible series of spectacular plays in a game that I'll never forget. I've been lucky enough to have attended 10 Super Bowls and seen other classics in person, such as the game where the 49ers clinched their first Super Bowl berth on that remarkable last-minute catch by Dwight Clark. However, unlike that 49ers-Cowboys title game of 1981 that coincidentally featured something like nine turnovers, I remember very few such mistakes in that first-round Raiders-Dolphins clash. This was football at its finest. It was Stabler throwing what legendary NFL Films announcer John Facenda would later describe as "butterflies" in tight coverage over the middle to sticky-fingered Fred Biletnikoff, or arching a long TD bomb to speedy wideout Cliff Branch. It was bruising running back Benny Malone of Miami fighting 23 yards for a go-ahead touchdown in the final two and a half minutes as, in the words of Raiders announcer Bill King, "He just bulled, smashed, and shoved defensive back Skip Thomas out of the way!"

But with the clock moving in short, tense bursts, Stabler coolly drove his team downfield against the Dolphins' vaunted "no name" defense, in what would be the classic Raiders comeback drive of the decade. Using the two-minute drill to perfection, Stabler found Biletnikoff several times on key second- and third-down plays, as the Raiders moved inexorably toward what King described as "the Promised Land."

Veteran backup Frank Pitts, a former standout with the old AFL rival Kansas City Chiefs, also came up big, making a crucial "heart-stopping, juggling catch" (as Bill King breathlessly described) to keep the drive going.

With the ball just eight yards away from the Promised Land (isn't that an apt description by King?), Stabler faded, looked, looked, and then was suddenly hit around the ankles from behind by charging Dolphins defensive lineman Vern Den Herder. As he was falling forward, Stabler looped the ball toward a knot of players in the end zone, trying to zero his pass in toward running back Clarence Davis. Years later, Paul Warfield told me that Davis was the Raiders' "worst pass catcher," but not in this instance.

With defensive back Mike Kolen as well as two of his Dolphins teammates vying for the airborne football, Davis somehow reached through this "sea of hands" and came down with the ball, tumbling into the end zone in a pile with the other Dolphins. An incredible score that put the Raiders ahead 28–26!

Yet the Dolphins and their great quarterback Bob Griese did not become two-time champs by giving up. Miami only needed a last-second field goal to win, and there were still 26 seconds to go. But Griese's first pass attempt was picked off by gritty linebacker Phil Villapiano, and a playoff victory was secured. In the locker room afterward, Miami coach Don Shula, normally the picture of stoicism, broke down and cried, he was so disappointed. It was the end of an era for the short-lived Dolphins dynasty, but for the Raiders, it was only their eighth year in a 20-year run of contending teams from the mid-1960s through the mid-1980s.

I remember sitting in traffic with my dad on the way home, elated and still a bit out of breath as we listened to radio color analyst Scotty Stirling review Bill King's memorable highlight calls of that unforgettable game. To me, that's what the Raiders were all about!

I trust, then, that you'll enjoy reading more stories of this legendary team in Steve Travers's fine book!

—Bruce Macgowan

ACKNOWLEDGMENTS

Thanks to Tom Bast, Amy Reagan, Alex Lubertozzi, Jess Paumier, Kelley White, Linc Wonham, Jennifer Barrell, Adam Motin, Laine Morreau, Morgan Hrejsa, Scott Rowan, Don Gulbrandsen, and all the great folks at Triumph Books and Random House Publishing, for having faith in me with this as well as numerous other books I have partnered with them to write. Thanks also to Craig Wiley, and to Peter Miller of the PMA Literary and Film Agency in New York City. Thank you to Lloyd Robinson of Suite A Management in Beverly Hills, as well. Thanks also to longtime *Oakland Tribune* photographer Ron Riesterer.

Thanks to some fellow Trojans who were also Raiders: Clarence Davis, Mike Rae, Manfred Moore, Justin Fargis, Marcus Allen, Ronnie Lott, Al Davis, Vince Evans, Lane Kiffin, Charles Phillips, John Vella, Rod Martin, Rod Sherman, Rodney Peete, and Todd Marinovich (among others). I also want to thank two Fighting Irish who were distinguished Raiders: Steve Beuerlein and Tim Brown. Alex Jacobs and Kevin McCormack, friends and longtime Raider fans: thanks for your help, insight, and opinions. Bruce Macgowan, when it comes to Bay Area sports, I defer to you, my friend. Thank you.

Of course, my thanks as always go out to my daughter, Elizabeth Travers; my parents, Don and Inge Travers; and to my Lord and savior, Jesus Christ, who has shed his grace on thee, and to whom all glory is due!

INTRODUCTION

Sportswriters are assigned stories and books all the time. It can be a mercenary process, diving into the glories and colorful history of a team or player the writer may not particularly care about or root for, much less have grown up with. Not so with this book.

This is a personal story. It starts in January of 1968. I was a young child, but in that past year for the first time I had started to follow sports. I rooted for a superstar tailback at the University of Southern California named O.J. Simpson. Then I heard about this thing called the "Super Bowl." I knew it was a very, very big deal.

Growing up in Marin County, California, I knew where Oakland was. I knew they had a football team called the Raiders, and they were playing in the Super Bowl. It was amazing to me that a team so close to where I lived was involved in something the whole world paid attention to.

The Raiders were playing the *Greenbrae* Packers, and I wondered, Where is the stadium? At the Bon Air Shopping Center? Greenbrae, you see, is an unincorporated section of Marin. They had recently built a nice shopping plaza there. It was, and still is, called Bon Air. But my father informed me the Raiders were not playing the Green*brae* Packers, but rather the Green *Bay* Packers, and that the Pack was *very good!*

The Raiders lost, but I was hooked. The 49ers? I could care less about them. The Raiders were my team. I rooted for East Bay clubs. In the baseball season, I was an A's fan. If you followed Bay

Area sports in those days, you listened to Bill King. He broadcast the Raiders and the Warriors.

Home games were never televised. In 1970, the Raiders had a memorable season. The ancient George Blanda came off the bench to save a remarkable number of games with miracle comebacks and field goals. The *most* memorable was a kick with the clock winding down to beat Cleveland 23–20. As the ball sailed through the uprights, Bill King declared that, "George Blanda is *king of the world!*" I'll never forget that as long as I live.

Blanda and his story play into that very unique chapter known as the "Raider way." The Raiders of the 1960s, 1970s, and early 1980s were the winningest team in pro football. They were not the best team. The Pittsburgh Steelers won more Super Bowls. Over time, Dallas and Green Bay laid an equal claim on football greatness. But the Raiders, in large part because of Blanda, were perhaps the most exciting, truly fantastic football team…ever.

The Raiders form the nucleus of a golden age of sports. New Yorkers often speak wistfully of their golden age—the 1950s—when each team had a superstar center fielder: Mickey Mantle of the Yankees, Willie Mays of the Giants, and Duke Snider of the Dodgers. In addition, Frank Gifford led the New York (football) Giants to glory. But New York never sniffed the great joy of being a California sports fan from the late 1960s to the early 1980s. These were my formative years.

I rooted for the Raiders (three Super Bowl titles), the A's (three World Series championships), the Warriors (one NBA title), the USC Trojans football team (four national championships), and John Wooden's UCLA basketball team (10 national championships). Almost every California team was good: the 49ers, the Rams, Stanford, the Dodgers, and the Lakers.

Baseball was the sport I was good at playing. In my senior year at Redwood High School, we traveled to San Diego to play Point Loma, Hoover, and Lincoln. We were told Lincoln's third baseman was "a boss football player." His name was Marcus Allen, and he could hit, too.

The Raiders' move to Los Angeles hurt a lot of folks in the East Bay, but not me. I was a student at the University of Southern

California, and attended a number of big Raider games at the nearby L.A. Memorial Coliseum. They seemed like the same old Raiders I knew and loved.

I had a personal connection to the L.A. Raiders. One of my best friends, Bruno Caravalho, bought the California Pizza and Pasta Company (also known as the "502 Club"), a longtime Trojan hangout located across the street from USC. As a young man, I managed the "Five-Oh." On Sunday afternoons after Raider home games at the nearby Coliseum, there was no spot in Beverly Hills or the Westside that was trendier to be at than the "Five-Oh."

All the Raider players would come in after the games, but what made it so hot was that all the *Raiderettes* came in, too. All I can say is that if the NFL had a non-fraternization rule barring cheerleaders from hanging out with the players, it was ignored much the way Al Davis ignored most of Pete Rozelle's edicts.

Word spread, and most of USC's football players would come in, too, which caused a lot of angst with the 'SC coaching staff. Things got pretty wild in that place. Use your imagination, and it probably happened.

After a few hours at the "Five-Oh," the Raiders and the Raiderettes would caravan down to the Red Onion in Redondo Beach, or some other South Bay dance spot. I lived down there at the time and would get invited by Bruno to come along. I remember hanging out with Rodney Peete, Steve Beuerlein, Marcus Allen, and all those guys. Good times, man.

I knew Todd Marinovich very well, when he was at USC and later with the Raiders. He would invite everybody to parties at his place on Manhattan Beach strand. I liked Todd, but it did not take a genius to see the guy lacked the dedication to be a big-time pro quarterback.

But if off-field partying did in Marinovich, he could hardly be blamed. That was Raider tradition. In his mind, it was the way Kenny Stabler had done it; the way Tooz and Alzado had done it.

This is what makes the Raiders so unique. Eventually, Art Shell put an end to the Raiders' "traveling cocktail parties." Stacey Toran was killed in a drunk driving auto accident, and society became less tolerant of aberrant behavior. Some have said this curtailing of the Raiders style explains why no Super Bowl victories have followed in the succeeding years.

The truth is, the Raiders won because they had some of the greatest players in the history of that most unique of all American games: pro football. This book tells those stories. It was a wild ride in the doing, and in the words of the late, great Bill King, you are "two yards from the Promised Land!"

The Autumn Wind is a Pirate,
Blustering in from the sea,
With a rollicking song,
He sweeps along,
Swaggering boisterously.

His face is weather-beaten,
He wears a hooded sash,
With a silver hat about his head,
And a bristling black mustache.

He growls as he storms the country,
A villain, big and bold,
And the trees all shake
and quiver and quake,
As he robs them of their gold.

The Autumn Wind is a Raider,
Pillaging just for fun,
he'll knock you around,
and upside down,
and laugh when he's conquered and won.

—Voiceover for the Oakland Raiders by Steve Sabol,
CEO of NFL Films, immortalized in recitation
by the legendary John Facenda

THE GOOD, THE BAD, AND THE UGLY
OAKLAND RAIDERS

STADIUM STORIES

THE SAN FRANCISCO RAIDERS?

They were an afterthought. A fill-in. A sub. A football team whose players had never met each other. An anomaly. They did not start in Oakland, and they were not the Raiders. They were the Señors. They started across the bay, in San Francisco.

First of all, the American Football League began in 1960. It was a fly-by-night organization, anyway, but the Oakland franchise was the fly-by-nightiest. There were eight original AFL teams. The Houston Oilers were owned by Bud Adams, a Texas...oilman, of course. They played at a high school stadium.

They were not the only team in Texas. The Dallas Texans were owned by the scion of an influential, highly conservative family: Lamar Hunt. But in 1960, the established National Football League added the Dallas Cowboys, coached by Tom Landry. The Cowboys were a disaster. The Texans, a success. Had they played each other in head-to-head matchups, the Texans or Oilers would have won easily, but in those early years the NFL had imprimatur enough to win the "battle of Dallas," thus creating the Kansas City Chiefs.

The Boston Patriots played at Fenway Park. The New York Titans played at the Polo Grounds. The Los Angeles Chargers toiled at the L.A. Memorial Coliseum, then at San Diego's old Balboa Stadium. The Denver Broncos played a mile above sea level. Every original AFL city was a political or economic hub except for Buffalo.

Then there was the Minneapolis–St. Paul franchise. Minnesota was entering the big time in 1960. The state had a long, proud football tradition. The Minnesota Golden Gophers of coach Bernie Bierman were a powerhouse rivaling Southern California, Notre Dame, and Alabama in the 1930s. Under Murray Warmath, they were again challenging for national championships in the early 1960s.

Metropolitan Stadium in Bloomington, located between the Twin Cities of Minneapolis and St. Paul, was going up. Calvin Griffith moved his Washington Senators there in 1961, setting up shop as the Twins. When the AFL started, they were the eighth franchise city, but at the last minute the NFL offered them a team. Thus were the Minnesota Vikings born, and Oakland became the last AFL city.

The Dodgers and Giants had successfully moved to the West Coast two years earlier. Charles O. Finley bid hard for the expansion Los Angeles Angels, but did not have the Hollywood clout of Gene Autry. After purchasing the Kansas City A's, he watched

TOP 10

California Championships Before the Raiders' 1960 Debut

	Team	Titles	Years
1.	USC track and field	20	1926, 1930–31, 1935–43, 1949–55, 1958
2.	USC football	4t	1928, 1931–32, 1939
	California football	4t	1920–22, 1937
4.	Stanford basketball	3t	1937–38, 1942
	Stanford football	3t	1905, 1926, 1940
6.	USC baseball	2t	1948, 1958
	California baseball	2t	1947, 1957
8.	Los Angeles Dodgers	1t	1959
	Los Angeles Rams	1t	1951
	UCLA football	1t	1954
	California basketball	1t	1959

closely the unfolding fortunes of the Raiders, eventually deciding to become their uneasy neighbor.

California supported four major-college football teams—Cal, Stanford, USC, and UCLA. The Minneapolis Lakers were moving to Los Angeles. The L.A. Rams and San Francisco 49ers had a lively rivalry. The Coliseum in Los Angeles was filled with 100,000 fans for big pro and college games. California was the future.

Therefore, despite not having a stadium—not to mention a coach, a staff, uniforms, a draft list, or a roster—Oakland was awarded the eighth AFL franchise on a "wing and a prayer." Actually, they assumed there would be a stadium, at least a temporary one. Oakland is located right next door to Berkeley, the home of the University of California. Their Memorial Stadium, built hazardously on top of the famed Hayward (earthquake) Fault in the lovely Strawberry Canyon, held around 80,000 fans. But by 1960, Cal-Berkeley was beginning to reject most of the things that make America great, among them free enterprise. As in mercenary professional athletes performing for pay "right out in the open," quipped writer Wells Twombly. They told the Raiders to take a hike.

Except, of course, they were not the Raiders. Chet Soda was an early financial backer, bound and determined to bring pro football to his city and give it some "big league" grandeur. He greeted everybody he met, "Hello, *señor*," much the way Babe Ruth called everybody "Keed" or USC baseball coach Rod Dedeaux dubbed everyone "Tiger." A nickname contest was held, and the team was called the Señors.

Without use of Memorial Stadium, the Oakland franchise had no place to play. They swallowed their pride and decided to use Kezar Stadium in San Francisco. Kezar was already an ancient edifice by 1960. Built for high school football, it held some 59,000 fans and had sold out its capacity for big games between Lowell, Balboa, St. Ignatius, and other schools in its heyday—the 1920s and 1930s. College football, TV, and the San Francisco 49ers stole the thunder from the preps and small colleges like USF and St. Mary's. The 49ers were a solid NFL franchise by 1960. Originally a member of the old All-American Conference, they and the Rams had been incorporated into the NFL by the early 1950s. The Rams managed to win the NFL title in 1951. The 49ers were always a day late and a dollar short, such as in 1957 when they blew a large lead in the second half of a playoff game against Detroit. Still, they were a contender. The 49ers and the city of San Francisco regarded *anything* from Oakland as decidedly low rent, second rate, minor league. As "lost generation" writer Gertrude Stein had once said of Oakland, "There is no there there."

The Oakland Señors...?

Soda decided their uniform colors would be red. Their "mascot" would be a Mexican sombrero. As soon as the Señors' name was introduced, it was rejected. One member of the Oakland City Council had attended Texas Tech University, the home of the Red Raiders. The colors were rejected, and the "Red" was taken out of the name. "Raiders" seemed a fit, since Oakland was a port city, home to many a ship's captain and seaman. One-time resident Jack London was an adventurer, and the image of "sea pirates" was romantic, fitting to the town.

With the rejection of "red" from the color scheme as well as the name, black seemed a natural to go with "Raiders," emblematic of the "black-hearted" ocean dwellers of Robert Louis Stevenson fame. All of this happened very quickly. Oakland was awarded the Minneapolis–St. Paul franchise a mere three weeks prior to the first scheduled exhibition game versus the Dallas Texans. The team was in an immediate hole. Because of the confusing last-minute developments, they had drafted late. They had no organization. All the best college players were gone to the other teams. The first exhibition was played on a typically cold, foggy San Francisco night in July of 1960.

DID YOU KNOW...

That after Minnesota went to the NFL instead of the AFL, the league briefly flirted with Atlanta before deciding to put the last of the original AFL teams in the Bay Area?

"I wonder how many people who saw that first game against the old Dallas Texans thought the Oakland Raiders would be around in the year 1973?" asked Jim Otto, a member of the original team, in Wells Twombly's *Oakland's Raiders: Fireworks and Fury* (1973).

Twelve thousand people are recorded to have been at Kezar that night. Very few of them paid for a ticket. The team had provided free or cut-rate tickets to anybody who wanted them.

The game, however, was prophetic. Dallas led all the way. With 1:22 to go, Oakland scored to narrow the gap to 14–13, Texans. They went for a two-point conversion but were stopped inches short. According to Otto, the fans still remaining were on their feet, cheering. A star was born!

DADDY DEAREST: AL DAVIS AND THE OWNERSHIP GROUP

After "war" broke out between the AFL and NFL, thus spooking the Minnesota group from taking up with the new league—then accepting an NFL expansion team instead—an ownership group from Oakland was needed in order to buy the new team. No one rich businessman stepped forward. Instead, eight men formed the ownership syndicate. The costs and aggravations of such an endeavor, combined with the natural power struggles and political intrigue inherent therein, thus reduced the eight-man to a fairly stable three-man group consisting of Wayne Valley, Ed McGah, and Robert Osborne.

The team was terrible in the beginning. Coach Eddie Erdelatz, who had enjoyed success at the Naval Academy in the 1950s, was unable to harness the mercenary pro game. After losing the first two games of the season by scores of 55–0 and 44–0, he was confronted by Valley, a millionaire construction magnate who had played fullback at Oregon State. When Erdelatz offered no plan, he passed from the scene and a reorganization ensued.

The *Oakland Tribune* offered constant speculation that the Raiders would move to Philadelphia, Atlanta, Chicago, Duluth....Without a stadium in Oakland, the situation would have to change. Candlestick Park was built for the Giants. The Philadelphia Warriors moved to the Cow Palace and created uniforms that said simply "The City." The Republicans decided to hold their 1964 convention in The City. San Francisco had everything.

Finally, the Raiders were able to move out of San Francisco when Frank Youell Field was hastily constructed. It was a temporary fix—a high-school-quality field built on what is now a parking lot adjacent to the 880 Freeway, next to Laney College. Youell Field would not do over the long haul, but with further plans to build the Oakland–Alameda Country Coliseum, it would have to suffice until that ambitious project could be completed.

Next came the search for a coach. The failure to compete in the original draft had set the team's roster way back. In 1962, the team hired and fired several coaches. Valley interviewed every available prospect. They all turned down the job, citing the lack of talent stemming from the first draft, followed by failure to sign players drafted in subsequent years.

Finally, Valley approached Al Davis, a 33-year-old assistant on Sid Gillman's staff with the San Diego Chargers. Davis was an unlikely "football genius." He was a non-practicing Jew who, while growing up in Brooklyn, New York, studied the way Adolf Hitler had conquered Europe. It would not be fair to say Davis admired Hitler, but Davis had a military mind and *did* admire the bold planning and execution of the German blitzkrieg. He translated this kind of "aerial bombardment" into his vision of what constituted the most effective form of football warfare.

Davis had a perfect football/military mind. His early years saw a combination of the two. He had no athletic talent but was captivated by football. Later Raider press guide biographies called Davis a "star" football player. Not true. He *may* have played freshman football in college. He attended Syracuse University. One story that made the rounds had Davis signing on as the Syracuse football team's student manager. When the team photo was taken, Davis managed to place himself on the row with the coaches, not with the student managers. Then he supposedly bribed the school yearbook staff into writing that he was an "assistant coach." Armed with this "evidence," he sent out résumés, looking for coaching gigs.

Davis did a stint in the Army, but somehow managed to use his military service—which was in the middle of the Korean War—to polish his football résumé, coaching the team at Fort

Al Davis was named the Raiders head coach and general manager in 1963 at the young age of 33. He immediately made his mark, leading the team to a 10–4 record and earning AFL Coach of the Year honors.

Belvoir, Virginia. After the service, he managed to land a job on the staff at The Citadel, a leading military school.

In no time, Davis engendered great anxiety, getting the school into trouble over his aggressive recruiting tactics. A firestorm of controversy surrounded him, causing the head coach to quit. Despite being the *reason* the coach quit, Davis had the chutzpah to march into the office of the Citadel president, General Mark Clark.

Clark was a living military hero surpassed at that time perhaps only by Dwight Eisenhower, Omar Bradley, and Douglas MacArthur. He had led the winning Italian campaign, liberating Rome in World War II. He looked at the odd Davis, who tried to

STADIUM STORIES

Stadiums the Raiders called home include Kezar Stadium, San Francisco (1960); Candlestick Park, San Francisco (1961); Frank Youell Field, Oakland (1962–1965); Oakland–Alameda County Coliseum (1966–1981, 1995–present*); L.A. Memorial Coliseum (1982–1994).

*Known as Network Associates Coliseum (1999–2004), McAfee Coliseum (2005–present).

score points by telling him he had named his child, Mark Clark Davis, after him, and then demanded that he be named the head coach. General Clark hemmed and hawed. Davis asked him, "Don't you want to win?"

"Of course I do," said General Clark, "...but not at any cost."

Thus was Davis shown the door. Remarkably, he eventually landed at one of the most prestigious programs in the nation. Don Clark hired him at the University of Southern California because Davis promised—and delivered—three football transfers from The Citadel, all of whom became starters at USC. It was a tough period at USC. The team, coming off a payola scandal that landed them on NCAA probation, struggled. Davis, however, was a colleague of future 'SC head coach John McKay, and legendary taskmaster Marv Goux. Davis tried to position himself as USC's next head coach when Clark left, but when McKay got the job, he was not invited to stay on.

Upon Clark's (and Davis's) departure, coinciding with the birth of the AFL in 1960, Davis managed to talk his way onto Sid Gillman's staff with the Los Angeles Chargers. The Chargers wanted to sign former UCLA quarterback Ronnie Knox to play quarterback, but Knox was a peripatetic personality not suited for pro football. They settled instead for future Congressman Jack Kemp, out of L.A.'s Fairfax High and Occidental

TRIVIA

Who was Frank Youell, the man Youell Field was named after?

Find the answers on page 177.

College. L.A. did not take to the Chargers. Tiny crowds at the 100,000-seat Coliseum were pitiful and embarrassing, so they packed their bags and took their act to San Diego.

The eventual success of the AFL is directly attributable to Gillman, the high-flying Chargers, Kemp...and Davis. They lit up the San Diego sky with a new brand of football, an embellishment of Gillman's genius and Davis's vision of "aerial bombardment."

Davis, a Svengali personality, talked Lance Alworth into signing with the Chargers instead of San Francisco; Keith Lincoln with the Chargers instead of Chicago; and USC All-American lineman Ron Mix with San Diego instead of Baltimore.

Still, "I wasn't that sure about him," Valley recalled. "I had heard he was too aggressive and that he'd do anything to win. I thought to myself, 'What do we need most?' The answer was: a winner. I guaranteed him he'd have the money he would need."

> "BLITZKRIEG. EXPEDIENCY. PANZERS. WEHRMACHT. QUICK STRIKE. BANG. BOOM. I ADMIRED THEM. I FELT THEY HAD SOMETHING....I DIDN'T HATE HITLER. HE CAPTIVATED ME..."
>
> —AL DAVIS ON THE NAZIS IN THE MAY 1981 EDITION OF *INSIDE SPORTS*

Davis was not from an impoverished background. He did not require a big salary, and at first rejected Valley's offer, explaining that he did not need the money, already had a good job with excellent compensation working for Gillman, and, "I don't think you'll spend the necessary money to build the kind of organization that I want."

Here was an ambitious young assistant football coach *turning down* the chance to be a head coach, an unheard-of prospect. The selling job was not Davis convincing Valley, but the other way around—or at least that was the way Davis maneuvered it, all to his benefit. Valley offered a three-year contract. Davis agreed on the proviso that he be given total command, like Hitler in Germany. The Raiders would be no democracy. The entire front-office staff was shown the door. The ticket manager was fired, replaced by the Chargers' man.

IF ONLY...

Al Davis had been made head football coach at the University of Southern California in 1960 instead of John McKay, the fortunes and identities of the Trojans and Raiders would have been far different than what we came to know.

"Poise is the answer...pride and poise," Davis told his players. "Wherever you go, you are the Oakland Raiders. Anybody who is ashamed of that can get an airplane ticket right now. I don't care who you are or what you've done. You're here now and you're going to win, win, win."

"It was like the young Alexander meeting the Macedonian army for the first time," wrote Twombly. The historical military comparisons would go on forever: Hitler taking Poland, Alexander conquering Asia Minor, Patton's drive through the Low Countries, Hannibal crossing the Alps, or Caesar's defeat of Pompey...these examples of dominance would be used countless times to describe "the Mad Bomber" Daryle Lamonica, the field generalship of Kenny Stabler, the bravado of Jim Plunkett in the face of his enemies.

The first thing Al Davis did when he took over as the Raider coach was to give the team a new look. They took the field in silver and black uniforms and a logo of a pirate's head wearing an old-fashioned maskless football helmet with an eye patch over his left eye, with two swords crossed in back, on a black shield with "Raiders" written in white above him. With the new look, the Raiders won their first game over the Oilers in Houston, 24–13, and also their second game a week later.

THE GOOD

FOOTBALL'S NAPOLEON

The period from 1963 to 1965 is pivotal in the history of the Raiders franchise. The team was set up for failure from the beginning. They called themselves the Oakland Raiders, but had played their games at Kezar Stadium and Candlestick Park in San Francisco. Then they moved into Youell Field—named appropriately after an undertaker—which was little more than portable stands. They were in debt, went through a succession of coaches, and could not attract any big names to take over. They missed the first draft and had little talent.

Then along came Al Davis! Davis played his cards just right, indicating that he liked his job with Sid Gillman in San Diego, did not need the money, did not respect the Raiders, did not feel the owners would commit themselves to building a champion...

Davis, the man who studied Hitler, the man who used military history and politics as his guideposts, certainly did just that in 1963. Julius Caesar portrayed himself as the only man who could unify a divided Roman Empire, but only if the senate would grant him dictatorial powers. Napoleon had done the same thing after the French Revolution. Hitler had

TRIVIA

How many times has a Raider been voted league Player of the Year or MVP?

Find the answers on page 177.

declared himself the savior of Germany after World War I, annexing Austria and making it clear that Teutonic glory would be theirs...only if he were allowed to implement his policies in an unimpeded manner.

In many ways, Wayne Valley played the President Hindenburg role, ceding control of the flailing "Weimar Republic" to Davis's New Order. However, when all is said and done, none of these grandiose comparisons with history would amount to a hill of beans had Davis not succeeded in a big way. In this respect, he lives up to the "genius" label that has been accorded him. His way was different. His way was successful. There is little if any luck involved. Davis had the vision, implemented it, willed it to victory.

Had Davis failed, and had the team continued on their downward slide, sports history would have been much different. The Raiders franchise would have failed, and they probably would have folded or moved to another city. The Oakland–Alameda County Coliseum would not have been built. The AFL may not have survived, merged with the NFL, and become the model of sports success that it became. The A's never would have moved to Oakland, and neither would the Golden State Warriors. The "Home of Champions" would simply have gone on as Gertrude Stein described it. The West Coast would look different.

The Raiders were invented for little purpose other than to serve as a natural opponent ("rival" being too strong a word) for Barron Hilton's Los Angeles Chargers. The hotel magnate bought the Chargers, originally an L.A. franchise, to give the AFL some Hollywood glitz. Paris Hilton's grandfather knew little about football, but the name "Chargers" was good advertising for his new venture, the credit card, which he called the "charge card." When the Minnesota group opted out, the Oakland franchise was awarded in order to give the Chargers a West Coast opponent, cutting down on travel expenses. Lack of attendance at the cavernous Coliseum led to the move to San Diego, where the "Charger" moniker was morphed into the lightning bolt image. They were the class of the league, but when Davis left Gillman's staff to take over at Oakland, much of the reason for their success went with him.

BUSINESS COMES FIRST

What did Al Davis do after Arizona State running back Tony Lorick, drafted by Oakland in the 1964 Draft, signed instead with the NFL's Baltimore Colts? Two things. First, he vowed, "I'll never again lose a number-one pick." He never did. Then, the next year, he went after and signed another Arizona State running back, Larry Todd—who still had a year of eligibility—for the sole purpose of getting revenge on Sun Devil coach Frank Kush, who had talked Lorick out of signing with the AFL. Todd never developed, but Davis made his point.

Davis knew he needed to develop interest in the Oakland franchise. The 49ers were the toast of the Bay Area, but to Davis's delight, the 1960s were down years in their franchise history. Davis was able to distinguish the look and image of his team from his cross-bay rivals. If Davis could win, he knew that he could get Oakland to build a first-class modern stadium. With that would come the fan base, the money, and the success of a great sports franchise.

His first target was the *Oakland Tribune* newspaper. The *Trib* had a small circulation of about 200,000 and was considered an East Bay paper, paling in comparison to the larger *San Francisco Chronicle* and Hearst-owned *Examiner*. The *Tribune* was published by William Knowland, a conservative Republican U.S. senator, representing California in the 1950s. Knowland wanted to make his newspaper the West Coast version of *The Washington Post*. He failed in this endeavor, probably because the politics of Northern California, particularly that of the East Bay, differed from his editorial leanings. The West Coast "paper of record" label would not go to the *Tribune*, but rather to Otis Chandler's *Los Angeles Times*. They recognized the shifting political winds while moving from that of a Republican mouthpiece to a paper of international journalism with a sports page worthy of the region's rise in pro and college athletics.

But Davis knew that sports could propel a newspaper's circulation. He arranged a deal whereby the *Tribune* became the de facto arm of Raider publicity. Davis promised that all Raider stories would be filtered not to the *Chronicle* or *Examiner*, but to the *Trib*. It was a pure "I'll scratch your back if you scratch mine" arrangement, in many ways a first for the East Bay, which had always groveled for attention in an effort to get San Francisco to recognize them. No more. Davis represented the East Bay's new identity.

The *Trib* printed every possible Raider angle, and their readership lapped up all of it. In retrospect, however, this is a symptom more than a cause of the Raider success. Had the team been a loser on the field, nobody would have cared to read about the doings of their "stars." But in making the arrangement that he did, Davis saw to it that when the team *did* win on the field, it would not be a "shout in the wilderness."

Davis was in Oakland first, which partially explains why his team was so much more financially successful than Charlie O. Finley's A's of the 1970s. But Davis tapped into the Oakland psyche in ways Finley chose to ignore. Finley was an absentee owner who marketed his team as a circus act—something from the South with a touch of the old Negro Leagues, a bit of a clown act. Davis went for fear and intimidation, in confluence with the growing Hell's Angels and Black Panther movements that grew up side by side with the Oakland Raiders of the 1960s. They were blue collar, outsiders, rebels.

Again, however, none of that would have mattered had the team not won on the field. In this respect, Davis's skills in identity marketing or Napoleonic power-grabbing would not have mattered had he not backed it up with battlefield success!

"THE MAD BOMBER"

Daryle Lamonica is well known in Raider lore as "the Mad Bomber" because of his style of throwing the long ball. Lamonica and his team helped to revolutionize the game. What Knute Rockne and Sammy Baugh had done before them, the Raiders improved on.

The aerial game marked the difference between the AFL and the NFL. The older league had its share of great passers, of course—namely, Johnny Unitas and Sonny Jurgensen—but even those talented quarterbacks played within more restricted offensive schemes.

The Green Bay Packers dominated the NFL. Bart Starr was certainly a good passer, but the Pack played a conservative style, emphasizing the run to set up the pass. Many coaches believed passing was too risky. An incomplete pass netted zero yards, and of course an interception was disaster.

The AFL teams, however, went to the air with regularity. Sid Gillman started it. Al Davis instituted it. Daryle Lamonica perfected it.

Lamonica, interestingly enough, played at Clovis High School in Fresno. He grew up watching the Clovis Cougars do yearly battle with the Sanger Apaches. Sanger had a talented quarterback named Tom Flores. Flores went on to star at UOP, then helmed the Raider offense in the early 1960s.

"Tom started it all with the Raiders at quarterback," recalled Lamonica. "He went through some real tough years in Oakland, but when I got there, everything was in place."

That Howard Cosell gave Daryle Lamonica the nickname "the Mad Bomber"?

Flores ranks fourth in Raider history with 92 touchdown passes and set a single-game mark that still stands, with six versus Houston in 1963. In 1966, Flores passed for 2,638 yards and 24 touchdowns, but in the offseason, he was "shuffled off to Buffalo" in exchange for the younger man from the San Joaquin Valley, Lamonica.

For Flores, it was a bitter pill. The Bills, one of the stronger AFL teams of the early years, were on the descent. The Raiders, a joke in the beginning, were on the rise. Davis had seen Lamonica rally his team in relief of Jack Kemp and knew that he was the man to lead his team in 1967. Despite returning to his native California, Lamonica, who had played at Notre Dame, did not at first realize what a break it was for him. But, upon his arrival, Davis enthusiastically painted a portrait of what the Oakland offense could do under his leadership. Lamonica "got excited pretty quickly." Having his family able to see him play also was a plus.

Lamonica led the team to a 13–1 record in 1967. He was the best player in the American Football League. Whereas Kansas City had won the championship in 1966 and was Oakland's "Chief" rival, when Lamonica arrived he was the margin of advantage for Davis's team. His greatest season was in 1969, when he passed for 34 touchdowns and tied Flores's record with a six-TD game against the Bills. And between 1968 and 1970, he threw at least one touchdown pass in 25 straight games.

"It was an exceptional offense because we could throw deep to not only the wide receivers, but [also to] the tight ends and the running backs," Lamonica said. "Clem Daniels could come out of the backfield and outrun most defensive backs, and Al Davis turned Billy Cannon into a tight end who could do the same thing."

Lamonica went deep on either side of the field. If he was in enemy territory, he eschewed ball control, going for the end zone. His passing percentage was usually below 50 percent, which was immaterial to Davis.

"Our philosophy was attack, attack, attack," Lamonica said. He went early and often for Fred Biletnikoff, Warren Wells, and later Cliff Branch. After Cannon, Raymond Chester from Morgan State was brought in to great effect. Despite the seemingly "mad" approach, the Raider mindset was mathematical. The idea was to create 24 points out of seven or eight plays, which would be difficult to beat. Lamonica had a cannon arm, but the Davis scheme was the difference. Lamonica was not fast nor a good scrambler, but the tight ends and running backs available for outlet passes

TOP 10

Greatest AFL Quarterbacks

1. Joe Namath, Jets
2. Len Dawson, Texans-Chiefs
3. **Daryle Lamonica, Raiders**
4. John Hadl, Chargers
5. Jack Kemp, Chargers-Bills
6. **George Blanda, Oilers-Raiders**
7. **Tom Flores, Raiders-Bills**
8. Bob Griese, Dolphins
9. Pete Beathard, Chiefs-Oilers
10. Mike Taliaferro, Patriots

Daryle Lamonica—the "Mad Bomber"—helped revolutionize football in the late 1960s by quarterbacking the Raiders' pass-happy offense. This throw-first mentality helped push Oakland to a 13–1 record in 1967 and a berth in Super Bowl II.

meant that even if blitzed, Oakland could pull off a big play. However, the key to the Raiders' passing attack was born of necessity: the strong front line.

"The Raiders were the forerunners in stressing physical strength up front, and that emphasis has proved out," observed Dallas Cowboy coach Tom Landry.

Jim Otto had been with the club since 1960. His emergence as a star was not a sure thing. Otto was a workaholic who developed great strength in the weight room. Combined with intelligence and experience, he became one of the greatest centers in the game's history. But it was the emergence of Kansas City's 6'7", 280-pound defensive right tackle Buck Buchanan that created the urgency to stop him.

Davis realized his team would have to face Buchanan twice a year for 10 years. "We wanted to make damned sure we had somebody to line up against him," he said. "So in the first round of the 1967 Draft we selected Eugene Upshaw from Texas A&I and made him our left guard. He was 6'5", 255 pounds.

"Everybody said we were crazy because in those days they were using short, squatty guards. I wanted big men up front to protect the quarterback."

It was the presence of protectors like Otto and Upshaw that gave Lamonica the extra split second to find an open man, but it was his own "poise" in the pocket that allowed him to make maximum use of speed—in the case of Wells—or moves, as in the case of Biletnikoff.

Lamonica was not an extraordinarily big man, but he was tough, willing to take a hit after he released the ball. It paid off, time after time. He took some criticism, however, mainly because he never won the ultimate "big game," a Super Bowl. Lamonica led his team to many great victories by large margins, but lost clutch games, too. The 1968 Super Bowl was one, although, at least on that day, the Raiders were outmanned. His "fumbled lateral" against the Jets in the 1968 AFL title game ruffled feathers. Lamonica was seen as having lost in a head-to-head confrontation with Joe Namath, even though he passed for 401 yards on a blustery afternoon at Shea Stadium.

His hand injury against Kansas City in the 1969 AFL championship game is less remembered than his failure to move the team in a low-scoring loss. In 1970, when the AFL and NFL merged into inter-conference play, Lamonica and his team fell, prompting many to say the game, now dominated by fancy defensive schemes designed to prevent his long-ball style, had passed them by.

Indeed, the great Raider comebacks and ultimate Super Bowl victory came with Ken Stabler—less physically gifted but considered a "gamer"—at the controls. Nevertheless, Lamonica remains a Raider great. He was exciting and extraordinarily successful.

DOUBLE ZERO

Jim Otto *is* the Oakland Raiders. Others are more famous or glamorous. None is more respected. No less a source than Al Davis considers him the ultimate Raider. He played his college ball at the University of Miami, long before the Hurricanes were a power. He was no hot prospect at 6′2″, 205 pounds. The NFL gave him no look (the team he would have loved to have played for, the Green Bay Packers, passed him by), but the Raiders let him compete. He made the team and hit the weight room, building his strength until he weighed 255 pounds.

On a bad team in 1960, Otto worked his way into the starting lineup, earning AFL All-Star recognition. Later, when the National Football League called to inquire of his services, Otto remained faithful to the team that gave him a chance. He made All-AFL every year and, in 1969, was named to the All-Time AFL team. He made All-Pro three years in a row after the Raiders joined the NFL. He started in 210 straight games. Including preseason, postseason, and all-star games, he played 308 games as a Raider. He

IF ONLY...

The Green Bay Packers had not already had Jim Ringo at center, Jim Otto might have been drafted by his home-state team. A Wisconsin native, Otto went undrafted by the NFL. But the Raiders drafted him, and he went on to a 15-year, Pro Football Hall of Fame career, being elected to Canton in 1980.

Hard-nosed center Jim Otto (wearing his famous double-zero jersey) was the heart of the Raiders offense for the team's first 15 years. Along the way, he started 210 straight games and was named to the Pro Bowl 12 times.

was the last of the original Raiders with his distinctive "double zero" uniform number, representing his chances of success when he first broke in. He twice won the Gorman Award (1968, 1971) as the "Player Who Best Exemplifies the Pride and Spirit of the Oakland Raiders." He was selected to the 25-Year AFL-NFL All-Star Team, and was the third AFL player selected to the Hall of Fame, in his first year of eligibility.

Otto is to the Raiders what Ernie Banks was to the Cubs, Jerry West to the Lakers. He was an indispensable part of the great offensive juggernauts, which relied on his stalwart blocking in order to give Daryle Lamonica, George Blanda, and Ken Stabler time to throw deep. Otto was the face of the team in good times and bad. He embodies the deep love between club and city.

Otto took to Davis, inspired by his slogans posted around the Raider offices: "Pride and Poise," "Commitment to Excellence," and "Pro Football's Dynamic Organization." After his first year in Oakland, Davis sent players like Otto out into the community, as far east as Sacramento, and they furthered the team's fan mystique.

"That first winter, he had us out meeting people and promoting the team," Otto recalled. "We hadn't done too much of that in the first three years. I thought it was just to sell tickets, but it was more than that. We were creating a relationship with the fans. It was great for us and for them."

In 1963, Otto was shaken up, taking himself out of a game. Davis, the first-year coach, approached him and used psychology.

"When I was with the Chargers, we felt if we could get you out of the game, the rest of the team would quit because you are the leader of the team," Davis told him. Otto never again left the field under his own power when Oakland had the ball.

"What Al said to me became etched indelibly in my mind," Otto said. "I took a beating sometimes, but I stayed in the game. I didn't want to disappoint him, the fans, my family, or my teammates. I was the captain for 12 or 13 years, and I guess I was a leader.

"It was hard sometimes, especially because I had a chronic problem with my neck. I would get a stinger, and it would just about knock me out. But there was no way I was going to come

DID YOU KNOW...

That the Raiders are still waiting to retire their first number?

out of the game. What he said that one time was enough."

Otto had nine surgeries on his knees but never missed a start. After an exhibition game injury against Buffalo in 1972, team doctor Robert Rosenfeld examined Otto and declared his only option to be surgery, which this time would require missing games. Otto declined, offering to play in pain because, "If I'm not playing, they'll stop thinking of me as the Raiders' indestructible center and somebody else will get the job."

Otto played through the pain, even though the medial ligaments on the inside of his knees had tears. He had more damage up front. He just played in heavy tapes and bandages.

Otto paid for his dedication after retirement following the 1974 season. He was virtually crippled, unable to walk normally. He gave everything he had to the game, to his team, and to Al Davis. Davis sat with Otto at almost every home game, treating him with the greatest respect of all Raiders. Davis admired his loyalty above all things. In 1995, Otto was named to the front office for special projects.

Otto did enjoy success as an entrepreneur. He bought a Burger King franchise in Auburn, California. Motorists on their way to and from Lake Tahoe for years saw the landmark billboard of old "Double Zero" in his Raider uniform advertising his Burger King. The town, Auburn, was also perfect for Otto, a rural paradise set in the low mountains of the California gold country, surrounded by plenty of huntin' and fishin'. Simple, just like Jim Otto.

Most experts agree that the greatest center of all time is either Otto or Dwight Stephenson of the Miami Dolphins. Dave Dalby followed in Otto's huge shadow and did very well. He was the center when they won the Super Bowl in 1977, an elusive achievement that, sadly, neither Otto nor George Blanda ever won.

Otto also became a new kind of lineman, an intelligent big man, a thinker. He was the typical John Madden player, too. Madden calls them "big uglies." He was not pretty. He played in pain. He gave no quarter. Otto played in some of the greatest games of all time. The "genius" Davis or the coaching legend Madden never would have achieved half of their glory without players like Otto. The blue-collar mentality of Oakland suited him perfectly, and he became one of the truly beloved figures in Oakland sports history.

THE PROMISED LAND

The New England Patriots, led by coach Chuck Fairbanks, were the Raiders' opponents in their first-round playoff game. Oakland had home-field advantage throughout, a huge factor considering the prospect of playing in freezing conditions back east. Fairbanks, who revitalized Oklahoma's program after the departure of Bud Wilkinson, had led the Patriots from a 3–11 mark in 1975 to an 11–3 record in 1976.

The Pats were traditional AFL, and then AFC, patsies. There was little enthusiasm in Boston, a baseball town that was crazy for the Red Sox. But Fairbanks had quietly built a contender, centering his team around two old collegiate rivals. In 1970, USC's great black fullback, Sam "Bam" Cunningham had led Troy to a resounding win over Alabama in Birmingham, a game credited with ending segregation in Southern collegiate football programs. Cunningham's opponent at Legion Field that day was now his teammate. Offensive lineman John Hannah, an All-Pro, was now blocking for him, a fact that says much about the power of sports in the pantheon of social progress.

Echoes of that 1970 night in Birmingham rang louder also in the form of Raider stars Clarence Davis and John Vella, Cunningham's teammates at USC. New England quarterback Steve Grogan, who replaced the failed Jim Plunkett, was bound and determined to disrupt any "old home week" festivities. He had his team winning 21–10. Oakland had all the "bells and whistles" of a championship club, but the game seemed to be a replay of so many postseason disappointments of previous seasons—a critical letdown, a team overlooking an underdog opponent in anticipation of a hated foe.

But just as everything else fell into place in 1976, so too did

A gang of Viking defenders drag down Raider tight end Dave Casper during Super Bowl XI at the Rose Bowl. Casper caught four passes—one for a touchdown—as Oakland dominated Minnesota in the 1977 game, 32–14.

the Raiders in crunch time, courtesy of the great Kenny Stabler and a little bit of luck. Snake engineered a drive with two key tosses to Biletnikoff. When Mark van Eeghen scored from a yard out, it was 21–17, Patriots.

Oakland held New England and got the ball back for one final desperation drive, the Coliseum crowd begging, imploring, praying for Snake to work his magic one more time. Stabler drove his team down the field but stalled at the Patriots 27. Needing a touchdown, the former signal-caller for Bear Bryant—the Alabama-USC connections were everywhere—faced a third-and-18 situation with 57 clicks left on the clock. Should he try to get all 18 yards on one pass, or split the difference and face a do-or-die fourth-down play with time running out?

Stabler dropped back, facing a heavy rush from defensive end "Sugar Ray" Hamilton, who forced an incompletion but hit him hard. The flag fell, and the crowd went crazy when a roughing-the-passer penalty was assessed on New England, a play that is disputed to this day but, upon review, appears to be legitimate, albeit less than obvious.

Regardless, Stabler and his team were given new life. Snake was not to be denied this time, running it in from a yard out to win 24–21. His bootleg run was reminiscent of his scamper to "beat" Pittsburgh in 1972 before "the Immaculate Reception" ruined his day.

Pittsburgh loomed large over the landscape, like Hannibal occupying the Italian countryside. Coach Chuck Noll's team, led by superstar quarterback Terry Bradshaw, had come fully into their own after "the Immaculate Reception." Decisive winners of two straight Super Bowls, they were well established as one of the great teams in the game's history, their star-studded lineup dotted with players in their Hall of Fame prime. They were *the* great challenge of Al Davis's team. Few rivalries have been as heated.

Their early-season losses and untimely injuries had been overcome. The Steeler squad that beat Baltimore 40–14 the same weekend Oakland looked vulnerable against New England was apparently as good as any of the Pittsburgh title teams of the 1970s.

BY THE NUMBERS

5—The number of Super Bowls won by the AFC from 1973 to 1977.

11—The number of Super Bowls won by the AFL and AFC from 1969 to 1981.

But their two great running backs, Franco Harris and Rocky Bleier, were injured when Pittsburgh entered the Coliseum. In all the succeeding years, Pittsburgh fans and many players have felt that the healthy presence of Harris and Bleier—or at the least

Harris—would have been the difference, but that difference was substantial. The final score does not lend much credence to the argument, as Oakland stomped them by 17 points before a wild Coliseum throng, 24–7.

Without the ground attack to balance the offense, Bradshaw's aerial game, featuring talented receivers Lynn Swann (still another Trojan) and John Stallworth, stalled. Raider linebacker Willie Hall (USC) intercepted Bradshaw. Stabler hit Biletnikoff for 31 yards, spurring a 17–7 Raider halftime lead.

In the second half, Madden's team realized that they had the physical edge over Pittsburgh. They decided to go conservative. Pete Banaszak caught a short touchdown toss, the defense bottled up Bradshaw, and Oakland was headed to the Super Bowl after their 24–7 win.

The Super Bowl was just more serendipity in this perfect season: the home-opening comeback over Pittsburgh; every close regular season game going their way in a 13–1 year; coming back against New England; and a demonstration of Al Davis–style dominance over Pittsburgh.

Oakland, with a roster filled with USC Trojans, faced a team with a fair number of ex-USC players of their own, the Minnesota Vikings, at a location often called 'SC's "winter residence"—the famed Rose Bowl in Pasadena, for the championship of the world.

It was as if John McKay's 1972 national champs were "all grown up," taking their natural next big football step. For Davis, the former USC assistant who always admired that school and the pro quality of its football products, it was natural that his greatest team be populated by so many former 'SC stars.

On a sun-kissed Southern California Sunday, the huge throng was heavy with silver and black in a game played only six and a half hours by car from Oakland. The Vikings were overmatched. The AFC had firmly established itself as the superior conference one decade after Pete Rozelle's merger. First, the Jets and Chiefs had trampled the NFL's finest. When the leagues consolidated in 1970, the Super Bowl continued to favor the AFC. The only NFC team to win a Super Bowl was Dallas in 1971.

STADIUM STORIES

The 1977 Oakland-Minnesota Super Bowl was played at the Rose Bowl in Pasadena, the first time it was ever held at that location. Two Super Bowls were played at the Los Angeles Memorial Coliseum (Super Bowl I in 1967, and Super Bowl VII in 1973). In succeeding years, the game has never returned to the Coliseum. It has been played in California again; at the Rose Bowl, San Diego Jack Murphy Stadium, and Stanford Stadium.

The AFC featured three teams in the 1970s that were legitimate dynasties—the Dolphins, the Steelers, and the emerging Raiders. The NFC was defense-heavy. Dallas, led by quarterback Roger Staubach, probably had what it took to go all the way, and in truth are judged by history as a power matching the AFC's best, but the conference seemed to come down to conservative teams with little personality: the Rams and Vikings.

Los Angeles was a defensive juggernaut during the regular season, but seemed to fall apart in the playoffs. The Vikings had dominated with different quarterbacks in the late 1960s and early '70s, but now featured a legitimate star, Fran Tarkenton. In the 1976 NFC Championship Game, the Ram defense thought they could stifle Tarkenton and give (another USC) quarterback, Pat Haden, enough to give them a low-scoring win.

The football gods seemed to have it in for the Rams, however. The day after Christmas, the Rams got thumped by the Vikings, 24–13, in Minnesota, after having tied them during the regular season. The 11–2–1 Vikings earned the trip to a Super Bowl game played just half an hour away from the Rams' home field.

Minnesota showed up at the Rose Bowl, basking in the typical warm Southern California weather. It was the Vikings' fourth Super Bowl appearance in eight years. The closest they'd come in their first three tries was against the Steelers in Super Bowl IX, competing with Pittsburgh for three quarters before finally losing 16–6. This time the blowout would overshadow previous bitter losses.

BE TRUE TO YOUR SCHOOL

The Raiders have always had a strong USC connection, going back to Trojan assistant coach Al Davis, then Raider assistant John Robinson. But in the 1977 Super Bowl, no less than nine ex–Southern California players participated. For Oakland: Clarence Davis, Willie Hall, Manfred Moore, Charles Phillips, Mike Rae, Skip Thomas, and John Vella. For Minnesota: Steve Riley and Ron Yary.

When Minnesota blocked a Ray Guy punt and had the football within spitting distance of the end zone, they thought this might be their year, but the theme of the day was established shortly thereafter when halfback Brent McClanahan fumbled. Willie Hall recovered it.

Stabler, who liked to go deep on occasion, also went to the short game when appropriate, such as when his team's matchup superiority resulted in an old-fashioned butt-whuppin'. Like that day. He drove Oakland down the field using the run in sync with short, crisp passes. Banaszak scored from the 1, and they were on their way. Oakland just pounded on the so-called "Purple People Eaters," forging a commanding 19–0 lead. When the Vikes made their bid to get back in the game, scoring in the third quarter to trim it to 19–7, Oakland had a ready answer, driving for another Banaszak score, 26–7.

When Willie Brown picked Tarkenton and ran it back three-quarters the length of the field for a touchdown, it was all over but the shouting (the main duties of which were handled by Madden on the field and Bill King in the booth). Davis rushed for 137 yards. Art Shell and Gene Upshaw were at their all-time best. Stabler had as much time as a Christian waiting for the Second Coming. Biletnikoff, the recipient of Stabler's pinpoint passes and the "we can hold 'em as long as you need us to" blocking of Upshaw and Shell, earned MVP honors.

Final score: Raiders 32, Vikings 14.

"GUYS DO STUFF"

John Madden, who was inducted into the Pro Football Hall of Fame in 2006, coached the Oakland Raiders from 1969 to 1978. He never coached another pro football team, which makes him a rarity of sorts in the mercenary world of professional sports. He is and always will be associated with the Raiders, although nationally he is better known for his many years as a TV analyst. In all those years, Madden has remained a Bay Area guy, living in the exclusive Blackhawk section of Danville.

In keeping with his Bay Area persona, Madden has often been a guest, sometimes even a regular one, on various radio programs. In 1988 he was talking with Frank Dill, one of the morning show hosts at KNBR.

A pitcher for the New York Mets had recently sliced off part of his finger trimming the hedges at his house. Madden was asked if pro athletes should be prohibited from any kind of dangerous activities; not just motorcycle riding, but gardening, woodwork, basketball, or a million other "hazardous" things.

"Hey," Madden said, "guys do stuff. You can't prevent guys from doin' stuff like that."

If somebody else said it, it might not have sounded funny. When Madden says something, even if he is serious—which he actually is most of the time—it still sounds funny. He is like the late, great comic actor John Candy. He can just stand there and make you laugh without trying.

Madden is a Bay Area guy today because he has always been one. He grew up in the San Francisco suburb of Daly City, where he was a catcher on the Jefferson High School baseball team as well as a lineman on the football squad. He loved baseball and continues to be a big fan to this day.

His boyhood friend was John Robinson. Robinson went to Serra High, the Catholic school in nearby San Mateo (which also produced Barry Bonds and Tom Brady, as well as numerous other sports heroes).

In 1975, an arrangement was made between the Raiders and USC. Robinson was an assistant coach under John McKay at USC.

McKay planned to retire. USC wanted Robinson to replace him, but felt he needed head-coaching experience. John Madden hired Robinson to be an "assistant head coach" with the Raiders for one year, after which he was hired as 'SC's head man, where he won a national title and three Rose Bowls.

Madden played with another future Trojan coach, Ted Tollner, at Cal Poly San Luis Obispo. Tollner survived a plane crash that killed about half the people on board, including 16 of his players. This traumatic event involving many of his friends eventually had the profound effect on Madden's life of cutting his coaching career short and making him a bus traveler for the next 30 years.

Young fans may only know John Madden as a popular football broadcaster, but he was one of the top NFL head coaches of the 1970s. During his 10-year tenure leading the Raiders, the fiery Madden racked up 112 victories and a Super Bowl championship.

Madden got into coaching and found himself on the "fast track" at just the right time. The growth of the American Football League not only created opportunities for new coaches but also for new ideas. Madden had new ideas. He was hired as a Raider assistant and was on John Rauch's staff when Oakland lost Super Bowl II in 1968. In 1969, at the age of 33, Madden was hired to replace Rauch. Rauch had gone 13–1 and 12–2 the two previous seasons, so Madden's 12–1–1 record in '69 was par for the course.

HALL OF FAMERS

John Madden's lifetime pro football coaching record, all with the Oakland Raiders, is 112–39–7.

While some suggested that Madden was a "puppet" whose strings were pulled by Al Davis, Wells Twombly more accurately described in *Oakland's Raiders: Fireworks and Fury*, that "Madden is not a great egotist....He does not hold his job by trying to spread his shadow over everyone he touches. Al Davis is the chief executive and John Madden is the chairman of the Joint Chiefs of Staff. The two men cooperate perfectly, regardless of rumors to the contrary."

Madden saw Oakland through the transition from Daryle Lamonica to Ken Stabler, which had its share of bumps in the road but ultimately proved to be the team's greatest glory years. Madden was a workaholic, which explains why he went into broadcasting, a much less stressful occupation.

"I work 18 hours a day during the football season," he said in 1973. "I don't own a mountain cabin. I believe that a successful coach must be totally dedicated. I don't even play golf. If I don't give this job 99 percent, I'm a dead coach."

"There never was a name in my mind," Davis said of hiring Madden. "I wanted John. He has the same temperament as Walter Alston of the Dodgers. As I've said, the Dodgers find Dodger-types and keep Alston for 20 years. We look for Raider-types and we have an Alston-type to lead them. It's as simple as that, and people try to make it sound so complicated."

"A successful professional football club must, by its very nature, be an absolute dictatorship," Madden stated. "It can't be a

TOP 20

All-Time Greatest
Pro Football Coaches

1. Vince Lombardi
2. Bill Walsh
3. Paul Brown
4. Tom Landry
5. Chuck Noll
6. Don Shula
7. Bill Parcells
8. Bill Belichick
9. Curly Lambeau
10. Joe Gibbs
11. George Halas
12. **John Madden**
13. Hank Stram
14. Mike Shanahan
15. Mike Holmgren
16. George Seifert
17. Jimmy Johnson
18. Bud Grant
19. Marv Levy
20. **Tom Flores**

popular democracy. We strive for harmony and a meeting of the minds of athletes, executives, and coaches who all think alike. There is no place for a person who can't stand constructive criticism. There isn't any room for anyone whose feelings are going to be hurt. I'm the general on the field. Al is the leader. That's how things are. Things aren't bad."

Madden was the perfect Raider coach. Very few others would have tolerated the shenanigans of those teams. Imagine Vince Lombardi or Tom Landry putting up with the Raiders' training camp hijinks in Santa Rosa! Davis installed a practice field next to the El Tropicana Motel, which was little more than a glorified Motel 6. Nearby were various seedy bars. The guys in those places tended to be cowboys or Hell's Angels types. The women were rural party girls lookin' for a good time, or motorcycle mamas lookin' for a better time. It was perfect for the Raiders.

How the Raiders got ready for the season year in and year out amid all the drinking and revelry is a true mystery. It is also odd that a win-at-all-costs man like Davis tolerated it, but he and Madden sensed that amid the partying, bonds of togetherness and camaraderie were formed. It was also an era of strained relations between whites and blacks. The nightly forays were an interracial affair, and in Santa Rosa friendships and trusts were developed that somehow paid dividends on the football field.

It was as if the loose, relaxed party atmosphere carried over into the huddle, where Stabler never seemed to bat an eye no matter the situation. John Matuszak, Lyle Alzado, Fred Biletnikoff, Marv Hubbard, and many others partied in Santa Rosa, at the airport bar in Oakland, on the road...but they performed like champions on Sundays.

When the Raiders were in Santa Rosa, of course, "camp followers" would travel there to "party" with the team. While this of course meant "football groupies," it also included a fair share of male fans—biker types and otherwise. In this respect, the Raiders represented the last of a dying breed, something the Dodgers had been in Brooklyn. They partied with their fans, and their everyman image was embodied by Madden, who never gave the appearance of a martinet general or pious taskmaster, like so many coaches.

Today, this is virtually unheard-of. Pro teams live in a velvet-rope world of agents, celebrities, and party girls making themselves available to them. Average fans just watch with lustful jealousy from well beyond an arc of bouncers.

But once upon a time, the Raiders were Oakland's team, and Santa Rosa's, as well. John Madden, the kind of guy who would stop and have a beer or five with those average fans, was the rush chairman of an egalitarian brotherhood that formed one of the great football operations of all time.

Today, Madden is a cult figure for fans who see in him that last vestige of normalcy in a game of multimillionaire, drugged behemoths. He is still sought after to comment on his bus travels to NFL cities.

"Never eat at a Mexican restaurant near the highway," he states. "It's a bluff. It looks good on the outside, but the food's no good inside. Always find a greasy spoon in the town, after askin' around."

"THE GREATNESS THAT IS THE RAIDERS"

In January of 1981, Al Davis graciously accepted the Lombardi Trophy from Pete Rozelle. It was like Charles de Gaulle and Dwight Eisenhower pretending that the "free French forces" were needed to liberate France. The tense scene was defused when, in Churchillian manner, Davis told the media that it was his team's "finest hour," indicative of "the greatness that is the Raiders."

This time, having won a Super Bowl he was not favored to capture, he seemed to enjoy it, as opposed to his fatalistic approach to the 1976 championship, when defeat with his greatest team might have been too much to bear.

The Oakland Raiders had hired Brooklyn-born Al Davis in 1963. He built a dynasty in Oakland and identified with the blue collar East Bay fan base. He enjoyed stickin' it to San Francisco and the "wine drinking" 49ers. But he was never one of those Bay Area guys who thinks the sun rises and sets there.

When Davis made his biggest football moves early on, it was in Southern California—first as an assistant at USC, then under Sid Gillman with the L.A. and San Diego Chargers. He had lived in the Southland long enough to know that it is bigger, a greater market, than the Bay Area, particularly his niche of the Bay Area. He recognized that L.A. had star power—TV, newspapers, Hollywood—and a bigger "personality" on the national stage, one that rivals that of his native New York.

For these reasons, it should not have come as a big surprise that he coveted what he saw as the future in L.A. After all, one of his stated goals in his short tenure as AFL commissioner had been to break "back" into the Los Angeles market.

The Rams moved to Orange Country in 1980. UCLA made the switch to the Rose Bowl. The L.A. Memorial Coliseum, indeed the city and county proper, were more or less "vacant." Davis looked at this development, and to his militaristic way of thinking, it was lightly defended Normandy after Hitler had been duped into thinking the real invasion would come at Pas-de-Calais. Rommel would realize the error of this thinking soon, so time was of the essence! Davis's "blitzkrieg" of Los Angeles needed to happen in lightning-strike manner.

A bigger stadium, more fans, more merchandising, greater radio and advertising revenue—the persona of a city that could match his own. He fell for the glamour of Los Angeles—the Beverly Hills home, the show biz panache—and for a number of years the town embraced the Raiders. But in the end, Davis misjudged what he had in L.A. and learned what he should have known, which is that it is a frontrunners' town. The fickle fans of the Southland reserve whatever loyalty they possess ultimately for the Dodgers and Trojans. All others are at the peril of their record, which had better be worthy of the A list.

But Los Angeles was on the rise in 1982. The Olympics were coming. Most of the teams were good, and attendance was up. The Dodgers and Angels were contenders. The Bruins and Trojans were strong. It was the era of the "Showtime" Lakers. The timing was good for Davis, in that the Joe Montana–Bill Walsh 49ers era was just starting to capture the imagination in San Francisco, while Anaheim's Rams were down after years of success.

DID YOU KNOW...

That in 2001 this author asked Bill Walsh to name his biggest influences, and Walsh replied, in part, "Al Davis, who I consider a true football genius"?

It took some doing, as does any seismic event, but Davis finally made the move to the Los Angeles Memorial Coliseum. It was a bumpy first year for several reasons, but all in all a good one. First, the Raiders managed to draft USC's Heisman Trophy tailback, Marcus Allen. He was an immediate star. To have a player of that local caliber starring on the same field where he thrilled college audiences was a great advantage.

The down side came in the form of a player's strike that, like the baseball walkout of the previous year, took a great season and ruined it. Quarterback Jim Plunkett was comfortable in Los Angeles, maybe even more so than he was playing in the shadow of his youth, in which he was raised by two blind parents and had to live up to the exalted status of athlete/role model. In L.A. he was just another star in the constellation.

Allen was spectacular, and the Raiders were 8–1, but of course seven games were lost to the strike. There were playoffs, and the Jets upset Los Angeles at the Coliseum. Washington called themselves "World Champions" because they won the Super Bowl, but it was just an asterisked strike season.

> "A SUCCESSFUL PROFESSIONAL FOOTBALL CLUB MUST, BY ITS VERY NATURE, BE AN ABSOLUTE DICTATORSHIP....I'M THE GENERAL ON THE FIELD. AL IS THE LEADER. THAT'S HOW THINGS ARE. THINGS AREN'T BAD."
>
> —JOHN MADDEN

Nineteen eighty-three was, to quote the doorman of the Emerald City, "a horse of a different color." Another Trojan great, Don Mosebar, was drafted. Charley Hannah came over from Tampa, and Mike Haynes was acquired from New England after holding out there. UCLA's Dokie Williams became a starter, and Greg Townsend came into his own as a pass rush specialist.

No longer living in suitcases, commuting to L.A. for games, the Raiders began to enjoy their surroundings. They won at Cincinnati to open the season, 20–10. Marcus Allen led the way with an early score.

Houston came to the Coliseum and lost 20–6. Veteran quarterback Archie Manning was sacked five times. On *Monday Night Football*, the Raiders demolished Miami for most of the game, but Dolphin rookie Dan Marino showed a portent of things to come when he directed two late drives to close the gap to a respectable 27–14. When they defeated the Broncos and befuddled rookie John Elway (who did not look nearly as ready for the spotlight as Marino) 22–7, L.A. was 4–0 and riding high.

Allen sat out the Washington game with a hamstring pull, but the road loss was one of the most exciting games ever played. It was a battle between two "Year of the Quarterback" graduates. Joe Theismann's Redskins jumped out to a big early lead, but Plunkett threw an incredible 99-yard touchdown pass to Branch to get the team back in it.

Theismann suddenly lost his hot hand, and Los Angeles controlled the game, building a 35–20 lead, capped by Greg Pruitt's 97-yard punt return that left the D.C. fans bewildered. Redskin coach Joe Gibbs then replaced John Riggins with Joe Washington, who caught a 6-yard touchdown pass as Theismann led his team on a last-minute drive to pull out the incredible 37–35 victory.

The game made it plainly obvious that these were the two best teams in pro football. It was a preview of the Super Bowl. The Raiders hoped that the results would be similar to the 1980 season, when they lost on the road to the NFC champion Eagles, only to apply retribution in the Super Bowl.

Los Angeles went through a bit of a midseason slump. Kansas City fell, 21–20, only because Ted Hendricks blocked Nick Lowery's game-winning field goal try from 45 yards out, but against Seattle the Silver and Black committed eight turnovers in a 38–36 defeat. Plunkett was sacked eight times and threw three interceptions.

In a move that, upon reflection, seems incredible, Marc Wilson replaced Plunkett and held the position for four weeks! When he passed for 318 yards to lead L.A. to a thrilling 40–38 win over Dallas, it looked like the future was now. Plunkett was seen as a "stopgap" quarterback, albeit one who had been doing more than that for three years. Fullback Frank Hawkins gained 118 yards on the ground against the Cowboys, and Ted Watts's interception of a Danny White pass set up Chris Bahr's game-winning field goal.

Seattle came to the Coliseum and, in another game that looking back is hard to believe, beat up on the Raiders, 34–21. In the back of the minds of some Raider fans, however, was the memory of 1969, when Oakland beat Kansas City twice during the regular season to establish dominance over them, only to fall to the Chiefs in the AFL title game.

If Seattle and Oakland were to play each other in the postseason, the Seahawks' two wins over the Raiders could be good news and bad news for them. The good news, of course, being the knowledge that they *could* beat them; the bad news being that the law of averages was against their accomplishing this task three times in one season.

The Seattle game exposed Wilson, as he was intercepted five times and lost the halo of future greatness, thus putting the team, after a Wilson injury, back in Plunkett's control. The veteran righted the tilting ship, leading Oakland to five straight victories, ultimately giving them the division title over Seattle.

Kansas City, Denver, and Buffalo fell, with the Bronco win being the hardest, 22–20. Rod Martin continued to make big plays on defense. Todd Christensen established himself as a bona fide star. Marcus Allen was one of the best running backs in the game.

The defense took control in a 27–12 win over the New York Giants. On a Thursday night in San Diego, Oakland posted 42 straight points after the Chargers broke out to a 10–0 lead, with Christensen scoring three times, and Hawkins twice. At 11–3, the division was clinched.

With little left to play for—the home-field advantage looked to be secure—Oakland blew a 24–7 lead and lost to the St. Louis Cardinals 34–24. This meant the finale against the Chargers indeed was for the right to play in L.A. Plunkett, Allen, Branch, and Bahr spurred them to the 30–14 victory over the ever-dangerous Chargers of Dan Fouts. They were 12–4 with the "hammer" over the 12–4 Dolphins, whom they had beaten.

TOP 10

All-Time Greatest
L.A. Pro Sports Champions

1. 1972 Lakers
2. 1963 Dodgers
3. 1987 Lakers
4. 1983 Raiders
5. 2003 Lakers
6. 1951 Rams
7. 1965 Dodgers
8. 1985 Lakers
9. 2002 Angels
10. 1988 Dodgers

KINGS OF TINSEL TOWN

After two seasons at the Los Angeles Coliseum, the team had performed brilliantly, but a disturbing trend was beginning to make itself felt. Attendance at the Coliseum was disappointing.

With the best and most exciting team in pro football, Davis thought his team's reception would match the boffo enthusiasm heaped upon the Dodgers when they arrived in 1958. Davis envisioned sellouts of the 92,000-seat Coliseum, but found that big crowds responded more to the marquee value of L.A.'s opponent than they did to the "greatness that is the Raiders." With the Thursday deadline for sellouts rarely met,

BE TRUE TO YOUR SCHOOL

Raiders tight end Todd Christensen and backup quarterback Marc Wilson both played at Brigham Young University. One USC Trojan has been named Super Bowl MVP playing for the Raiders (Marcus Allen in 1984). Lynn Swann of Pittsburgh also won it in 1976.

home TV contests—such an important factor in developing a following—were not frequent, which hurt the team's public perception.

The Rams were still very much a part of the L.A. consciousness. Ex-USC coach John Robinson had a contender in Anaheim, where they played in a stadium viewed as more amenable to upper crust fans. Davis envisioned the Coliseum as it was for Trojan games, filled with upscale alumni, their "trophy wives," and *USCion* children in tow. Instead, the Silver and Black's fan base increasingly reflected the team's "criminal element" in the form of inner city fans who identified with the Raiders' color scheme and style, much the way gang members do.

But these problems were viewed as "growing pains" that would work themselves out. In 1983, the L.A. move was still a successful one—perhaps not as visionary as Walter O'Malley's, but a bold grabbing of market share which, unfortunately, Davis probably equated with Adolf Hitler's taking of Czechoslovakia.

The 10–6 Central Division champion Pittsburgh Steelers came to the Coliseum, which was now completely sold out. Lester Hayes established his presence with authority by picking off Cliff Stoudt and running it all the way into the end zone. Allen scored twice, and Mike Haynes was tremendous. All vestiges of the old Raider-Steeler rivalry were replaced by Raider dominance, and again in Davis's historical way of thinking, he had outlasted his hated foes from the Steel City the way Rome had outlasted Attila the Hun. The final score was Los Angeles 38, Pittsburgh 10. Stoudt took more hits than Tokyo during the firebombings, and as Davis liked to say, "The quarterback must go down, and he must go down *hard!*"

BY THE NUMBERS

9—The number of Pro Bowl appearances by Raider Hall of Fame cornerback Mike Haynes in the fabulous 14-year NFL career he forged after starring at Arizona State.

Seattle beat Miami on the road and came in as a wild-card team with confidence, having beaten the Raiders twice, but it was not to be this time. Rookie running back Curt Warner, who had led Penn State to a Fiesta Bowl win over Marcus Allen and USC two years prior, was stopped, and Allen got his revenge. Strong safety Mike Davis intercepted Seahawk quarterback David Krieg twice, while Marcus poured it on for 154 yards on 25 attempts. Frank Hawkins bulled his way in twice. The line of scrimmage was L.A.'s domain, and the sellout crowd was exuberant in celebrating the 30–14 pasting, sending their men to the Super Bowl.

If Al Davis's team could capture the "World Championship of Professional Football" in just their second year in L.A., it would match the Dodgers, who accomplished that feat in their second season (1959). Davis hoped that such a victory would establish his team in the city, giving them the dominant position over the Rams, a winning organization that had never won a Super Bowl.

When the Raiders demolished Washington 38–9, it marked the high point in the career of Al Davis and the history of his team. It certainly looked to be vindication for him, answering the many critics of his L.A. move. Looking back on that era, some 25 years later, it seems there were mistakes and miscalculations. Certainly, the Raiders had captured the city's imagination, and it seemed unlikely at that point that their hold on the pro football mentality of Southern California would lessen.

USC was entering the longest drought period in their hallowed history. Indeed, the following two seasons saw the Raiders field teams that competed at the highest levels. But there was no extra "good will," so to speak. Unlike the Dodgers and Trojans, whose fan bases are loyal through good times and bad, the Raiders found themselves lumped in with the Rams, Lakers, Clippers, Kings, Mighty Ducks, Angels, and Bruins. All of them have known greatness, in some cases ultimate greatness. They have achieved success at the gate and been darlings of the populace in one way or another, but find that popularity very much a "what have you done for me lately?" proposition.

None of that mattered on January 22, 1984, in Tampa, Florida. Super Bowl XVIII had all the "bell and whistles" one could hope for, with two storied franchises going after the biggest prize in the game. It matched the two-time Super Bowl–champion Raiders against the defending champs, the same Redskin club that beat L.A. in the fifth game of the season.

DID YOU KNOW...

That the first "Million Dollar Gate" in NFL history came in 1982, the Raiders' first year in Los Angeles? The Raiders and L.A. Rams played to a sold-out Memorial Coliseum crowd, with gate receipts topping the $1 million mark. The Raiders won the cross-town battle 37–31.

Joe Theismann's team was favored, having gone 14–2 and beaten Joe Montana and the great Bill Walsh 49ers in the NFC title game. The television executives and all those who like the excellent ratings produced by a close game were disappointed, however, because Los Angeles dispatched Washington early, leaving no doubt as to their superiority. It seemed impossible to believe Washington had beaten this team in September. It seemed impossible to believe the Silver and Black had been beaten four times, much less twice by Seattle.

The Raiders exploded, all of their pent-up energy and emotion channeled perfectly, harnessed by a ferocious defensive scheme, Plunkett's big-game composure, and Marcus Allen's bid for immortality. Nose tackle Reggie Kinlaw, plus linebackers Bob Nelson, Matt Millen, and Ted Hendricks, bottled Theismann and Company like ketchup at the Heinz plant. Unable to get his passing game going, Theismann went to John Riggins, but he was stuffed repeatedly.

In the first quarter, Derrick Jensen blocked a Washington punt and fell on it in the end zone. When Plunkett nailed Branch for a touchdown, it was 14–0, but the game was secured, ironically, by a mistake by the great Redskin coach Joe Gibbs. Just before the half, instead of running out the clock and taking it in to regroup, Gibbs had Theismann throw a swing pass to Joe Washington—just like the one he had burned the Raiders on in Washington back in September. Defensive coordinator Charlie Sumner saw it from a mile away. Reserve linebacker Jack Squirek, responding to Sumner's play-calling, stepped in front of Washington, picked it off, and waltzed into the end zone. It demoralized Washington, now trailing 21–3.

Many viewers turned off their TV sets at that point, but those who stayed tuned still have great memories of the second half. That is because Marcus Allen's incredible performance has lived on in NFL Films' immortality the way Bart Starr's, Joe Montana's, and the Steel Curtain's Super Bowl moments have been preserved.

Allen took a handoff on his own 26, a simple off-tackle, but the Redskins plugged the hole, forcing Marcus to reverse course and use his speed to burn the Redskins for a 74-yard touchdown run that was a thing of beauty. It was the longest run from scrimmage in Super Bowl history. It was Allen's second TD of the game, and he was stopped just short of a third. Chris Bahr added a field goal, and suddenly Tom Flores had won two Super Bowls in four years, which has the effect of making him the most successful coach in the team's great history, with all due respect to John Madden.

The Raiders outscored opponents 106–33 in the postseason. They were never challenged, unlike the 1976 and 1980 Super Bowl champions, both of whom faced major scares on the road to victory. It was a team of great talent: Plunkett, Allen, Howie Long, Lester Hayes, Mike Haynes, Todd Christensen, Rod Martin, and Vann McElroy. Veterans Bob Nelson, Ted Hendricks, Lyle Alzado, Dave Dalby, Mickey Marvin, and Henry Lawrence were still excellent players. With the likes of Don Mosebar, Greg Townsend, and Dokie Williams waiting in the wings, there was no reason to believe the club's future would not be bright.

While Plunkett was sitting on top of the world, Marc Wilson had shown flashes of brilliance. There was no sentiment to replace Plunkett with Wilson in 1984, but plenty of optimism that a smooth quarterback transition could be effected when the time was right.

THE BAD

MERGER

After World War II, a new league was formed to challenge the NFL. Featuring successful franchises in Los Angeles (the Dons) and San Francisco, the All-American Football Conference had its moments. In the end, it failed to merge, although the Cleveland Browns and 49ers did receive an invite (the Dons didn't), which brought major pro sports to the West Coast before Walter O'Malley orchestrated the Dodger-Giant moves of 1957–1958.

The American Football League succeeded where the All-American Football Conference failed, precisely because the AFL had Al Davis. It was a new era—an era of jet travel, of unprecedented American economic expansion and political-military dominance, a time of entrepreneurial capitalism and liberalized court decisions giving more freedom than ever to the free-ranging spirit of sports enterprise. The AFL was successful on and off the field. Several of the league's owners had the kind of money to take big chances. Buffalo owner Ralph Wilson had secretly invested in the Raiders, which helped the club weather its early debt woes. The AFL declared all-out war on the traditional draft-and-sign methods of the NFL, which like baseball had a form of "reserve clause" that made a player virtual property, first in the manner of his selection, then in its contractual inflexibility.

The AFL, however, instituted the "futures" draft of underclassmen in the college ranks. They treated their players more like

SMOOTH OPERATOR

Al Davis, as commissioner of the American Football League, successfully talked "half of the NFL's top quarterbacks to agree to join the AFL" in his short three-month tenure, according to the Raider media guide. These "earth shattering changes to the landscape of pro football" would have "forced the NFL to once and for all view the AFL as a legitimate league," leading "to a merger, that would bring both leagues together with a common draft and a year-end championship game."

valued employees in other industries who had the freedom to work where and with whom they chose, within the strictures of signed contracts.

"You attack their supply lines," Davis said of the AFL's "war" with the NFL. He and his league fought like tribesmen in the mold of the "Arab revolt" led by T.E. Lawrence in World War I, consisting mostly of the destruction of Turkish railroads. A large number of top NFL stars were "secretly" signed to "future" AFL contracts, meaning that when their deals were up with current teams they would jump to the junior league.

Joe Namath of Alabama had signed with the New York Jets out of Alabama for $400,000. Notre Dame's Heisman Trophy winner John Huarte was also inked for big dough. The lure of huge money was irresistible, demonstrating the newfound place of sports in the American pantheon.

By 1966, the NFL was ready to sue for peace. The AFL wanted the best possible terms. There was only one man who, it was felt, had the brass knuckle qualities to force the best deal: Al Davis.

Davis was at first uninterested in becoming AFL commissioner. He was the Raiders' coach, dedicated to building a champion. But the Machiavellian Davis saw the future. Becoming commissioner was not just a selfless job, albeit one with a nice $60,000-a-year salary plus perks.

Davis was against a merger with the NFL. But as commissioner, he could at least steer things in favor of his Raiders, and at the appropriate time leave the job and return to Oakland, flush with the advantages bestowed by him. He also wanted to expand the AFL into Los Angeles.

Davis knew the future lay in the Sunbelt—the West and the South. His L.A. years, three with USC and one with the Chargers, had made an impact. The Coliseum and its 100,000 seats, the huge populace, and the growth of television, radio, and merchandising rights, made it a gold mine. The Angels had expanded the near-limitless market to Orange County. Davis could envision a Los Angeles sports behemoth that would overshadow the Chargers in San Diego.

In some ways, the AFL used Davis. He was like the IRA to the owners' Sinn Féin. Davis was to hit below the belt and cause as much damage as possible. In the meantime, the AFL owners would negotiate from the position of strength that Davis's actions leveraged for them, like Henry Kissinger getting a triangulated peace deal with the North Vietnamese, Russians, and Chinese only after bombing the hell out of Hanoi. The result of this situation would result in a good deal for the AFL, the NFL, and Pete Rozelle. It would forever mark Davis as an outsider, a renegade, even though he was positioned to be just that by the owners.

Tex Schramm of the Cowboys and Lamar Hunt of the Chiefs agreed on a merger. Secret meetings between Rozelle with various AFL and NFL owners were held, unbeknownst to Davis. He did not want the merger and didn't realize that he was being used to help the process along.

That, on the Raiders travel itinerary, it says at game time: "We go to war"?

When the dust settled, the AFL and NFL merged. The two leagues would remain as is through 1969, when the AFL TV contract expired. An "AFL-NFL Championship Game" (the Super Bowl) would be played between champions of the two leagues, the first one at the L.A. Coliseum in January 1967. In 1970, the leagues would be reconfigured into the American and National Football *Conferences*, with several NFL franchises filling out spots in the AFC, featuring an integrated schedule of inter-conference games.

This was all well and good, but Rozelle and the AFL owners sold out Davis. First, there would not be separate "league presidents" of the AFL and NFL, as there was in baseball. Pete Rozelle would be commissioner of the whole shebang, all of which fell under the rubric of the National Football League. Davis, instead of being elevated to a position on par with Rozelle, was useful no more, and therefore would be out of a job.

But just as painful was that the agreement was hammered out without his knowledge or consent. First, the AFL would have to come up with almost $27 million in order to join the party, but the New York and Oakland franchises be forced to pay additional *reparations* to the Giants and 49ers, respectively, because they had "encroached" on their territories. This was not the half of it. The Jets and Raiders were to move to cities with no NFL teams by the time the leagues fully merged into the inter-conference AFC-NFC configuration.

A common draft was agreed on, too, instead of the separate drafts of past years. The AFL had underestimated its value. Everywhere the teams and the leagues could be compared up until 1966, they had the upper hand. They signed the best college players, had the most exciting stars, played the most colorful brand of offensive football, and had captured major media markets.

In New York, "Broadway Joe" Namath and the Jets were the toast of the town, playing at brand new Shea Stadium while the Giants toiled in losing fashion in a stadium named after the Yankees. The Oilers moved into the Astrodome. The winning Raiders moved into the Coliseum while the loser 49ers played in the archaic Kezar.

Davis was livid, and Wayne Valley was flabbergasted. The *real war* had only just begun! Over the next years, court battles would ensue. The Raiders and Jets both remained in Oakland and New York, respectively. Much of the original "indemnity" money to be paid by the AFL to the NFL, and by individual teams, was greatly reduced. But in what may have been the most

GOING CAMPING

In training camp, Al Davis would put 300 pounds of weights on his bed and sit down with a towel around his neck, pretending to be lifting when he was not, just so people would think he was into weight training.

important development, Al Davis was now, for all practical purposes, out of a job that he had contracted to hold for several more years. Instead of being a figurehead until his contract expired, he turned "lemons into lemonade."

Negotiations were entered into, and Davis maximized his position of strength. Valley, the Raider ownership group, and Davis contracted for Davis to become a *one-third owner of the team* for the rock bottom price of $17,500. Davis had a windfall ownership stake in a lucrative franchise for the 1962 price of the team, which of course was when they were in debt, floundering, and on the verge of extinction. That was *still* not all of it.

A 10-year agreement was reached, making Davis the managing general partner. Valley and Ed McGah became silent partners. Davis, like Napoleon at Versailles, was given total autonomy. He was the dictator.

SO CLOSE, AND YET SO FAR

There are very few teams in professional sports that have risen as quickly, and to such heights, as the Oakland Raiders of the 1960s. They started out as a "minor league," almost a semipro outfit—a laughingstock in a nothing town in a "wing and a prayer" venture.

Then they hired Al Davis. Then he became league commissioner. Then he became a part owner of the team, and almost overnight they found themselves on the very biggest stage of them all: Super Bowl II versus *Vince Lombardi's* Packers at the Sugar Bowl in New Orleans.

The Raiders were a 13–1 team in 1967. They devastated their

playoff competition and looked unbeatable. The Pack was 9–4–1 and, frankly, needed every possible bit of home-field advantage that the Wisconsin winter could provide in earning their trip. They looked old, over the hill.

The Raiders may have been the better team, but that is just speculation. They were psyched out and beaten soundly. At the time, it was a common belief that the AFL was not, to coin a phrase, "in the NFL's league." It is only in retrospect, when one studies the subsequent Super Bowl victories by the AFL's Jets and Chiefs, the Hall of Famers who came out of the young league, and the seamless integration of the AFL into the AFC, that one can judge the 1967 Raiders—and the AFL—fairly. At the very least, they can console themselves with the knowledge that it took one of the most hallowed dynasties in sporting annals to beat them.

The January 1968 loss to Green Bay, however, was the beginning of a long, frustrating ride in which the Oakland Raiders were one of the greatest, most exciting teams ever assembled, but for a decade played bridesmaid to brides from New York, Kansas City, Miami, and Pittsburgh. Year in and year out, it was "so close, and yet so far."

The Raiders' rapid ascension had a surreal quality to it. Champions came from major cities: New York, Los Angeles, Chicago, Boston. In Green Bay's case, they were a small town, but their pro football imprimatur was so long established that the Packer stars of that era were like the ghosts of a hallowed shrine.

Oakland? This was before the A's, before the Warriors. The team played more or less at *Laney College*, for God's sake. The building of the Oakland–Alameda County Coliseum, which was filled to capacity immediately in 1966, when the team went 8–5–1, at least gave the team a big-league stadium. Had they played Green Bay at the venerable Orange Bowl after toiling all year in front of the portable seats of Youell Field, that would have been too much.

Al Davis and his Raiders have had an up-and-down relationship with the city of Oakland over the years, but anybody who wants to say Davis did the town wrong needs to study this history. He absolutely put Oakland on the map. It is fair to say that, before

Raiders defensive tackle Tom Keating (74) zeroes in on Packers fullback Ben Wilson during Super Bowl II. The Raiders' appearance in the championship put their often-overlooked hometown of Oakland on the map, but they lost the game 33–14.

the Raiders played Green Bay in Super Bowl II, a sizable number of Americans had *never heard* of Oakland, California.

The 1960s were a golden age of quarterbacks. Bart Starr of Green Bay; Sonny Jurgensen of Washington; Johnny Unitas and Earl Morrall of Baltimore; Y.A. Tittle of the New York Giants; Roman Gabriel of Los Angeles; Don Meredith, Roger Staubach, and Craig Morton of Dallas; and Fran Tarkenton of Minnesota—all played in the NFL in that decade.

AFL rosters featured the likes of Joe Namath of New York, Len Dawson of Kansas City, John Hadl of San Diego, Jack Kemp of San Diego and Buffalo, and George Blanda and Pete Beathard of Houston.

Linebacker Dan Conners, a Penn State product, was one of the defensive stars of the 1967 Oakland team that went to the Super Bowl. He played for the Raiders from 1964 to 1974, earning trips to the Pro Bowl three times.

The 1964–1967 college classes offered more of the same: John Huarte of Notre Dame, Bob Griese of Purdue, Steve Spurrier of Florida, and Ken Stabler of Alabama.

In 1967, the very best of them, at least until the Super Bowl, was Daryle Lamonica of the Raiders, the AFL's Most Valuable Player. Lamonica replaced Tom Flores when Davis traded Flores and Art Powell to Buffalo for him. Warren Wells of Texas Southern was signed to take Powell's job.

Two Hall of Famers found their way to Oakland. Cornerback Willie Brown was obtained via trade. George Blanda was deemed to be an old man in Houston. The Raiders figured he could kick field goals and be Lamonica's backup for a year or two. Rod Sherman, who caught a famous touchdown pass for USC to knock Notre Dame out of the national championship in 1964, was a wide receiver. Gene Upshaw was the number-one draft choice out of Texas A&I. Davis was ahead of his time when it came to drafting players from traditionally black colleges. He knew that Southern segregation meant that those schools were hotbeds of talent.

The "head coach" was John Rauch, but he would be the first of many to discover that this title has an entirely different meaning under Al Davis than it does anyplace else. Bill Walsh left after one year as a Raider assistant. A new man was brought in: linebackers coach John Madden.

Dan Birdwell, Roger Bird, Dan Conners, Bill Miller, Carleton Oats, Hewritt Dixon...these were just a few of the 1967 stars. This was a team that rates with the early 1980s Dan Fouts Chargers as one of the most explosive offensive juggernauts ever assembled. They played in a league in which almost every team could light it up, and in the words of Ira Simmons in *Black Knight: Al Davis and His Raiders,* were "gods...on the green fields of the brand new Coliseum." The game has never seen anything quite like it since.

The 51–0 opening win over Denver typified Raider dominance. They won their last 10 straight to finish a gaudy 13–1. In the AFL title game, Oakland destroyed Houston 40–7, triggering a big New Year's Eve celebration at Jack London Square. In the Super Bowl, Raider mistakes combined with Bart Starr hook-ups with Boyd Dowler and Max McGee combined to derail the Silver and Black. They trailed only by 16–7 at the half, but when Packer great Herb Adderley intercepted Lamonica and returned it 60 yards for a touchdown, the rout was on, 33–14.

NO REPEAT IN '77

Near the end of the 1970 classic, *Patton*, the German intelligence officer assigned to General Patton's file, amid the chaos of a falling Berlin, stares at a photo of the all-conquering American.

"The absence of war will destroy him," says the German.

Indeed, the film switches gears, from the high-speed voltage of U.S. victory to Patton's melancholy reaction to it. With no enemies left to vanquish, Patton seems not to know what to do with himself. This appeared to have been Al Davis's mood after the "fall of Minnesota."

Pete Rozelle presented the Lombardi Trophy to Davis after the Super Bowl victory. He was surrounded by Jack Tatum and George Atkinson, two of the players who embodied the so-called "criminal element" critics said marred Oakland from true greatness.

But it was Davis's reaction to victory over the Vikings that was most telling. There was "pride," and there was "poise," but the Davis reaction to ultimate success, to finally "winning the big one," said much about the man. He had been working for this day during each of his 16 years in pro football—plus his collegiate career before that. For 14 seasons he had fought to build this little franchise in a hardscrabble city, a team that played its games at Frank Youell Field, out of the media spotlight accorded to the glamour towns, in the shadow of glitzy San Francisco.

His goal, to turn them into "a dominant pro football power," to use just one of the many phrases that sounded as much like Patton exhorting the Third Army as a football phrase, had been

SCANDAL

Oakland defensive lineman Ben Davidson made a brief foray into acting after retiring from pro football. He appeared in *Behind the Green Door*, an adult film produced by the infamous Mitchell Brothers. Davidson does not shed his clothes, however. He plays the bouncer at an exclusive Sausalito orgy club, admitting Marilyn Chambers into the party for her big "debut."

accomplished prior to 1976. Now, however, they were not merely a "power," a "dominant force," or a "dynamic organization." His Silver and Black were—and this is another Davisism—the *World Champions of Professional Football.* You can look it up, in Raider publications. Raider Super Bowl victors are not just "Super Bowl Champs" or "World Champs" or "NFL Champs." They are the "World Champions of Professional Football."

> **DID YOU KNOW...**
>
> That the Oakland Raiders passed on drafting Cal All-American quarterback Craig Morton reportedly because Al Davis was worried that he would be pressured into playing the local hero, who would make him "look bad" if he failed to live up to expectations?

One almost expects to read Davis's bio and, instead of seeing him listed as the "principal owner and president of the organization with pro football's winningest percentage," to read instead "Al Davis, He of the Greatest Mind in Professional Football, Caesar of the Mightiest of All Grid Empires, and Master of All He Surveys in the Lands of the East Bay, the Central Valley, the Los Angeles Basin, and in That Most Hallowed of All Victorious Annexed Countries: The Raider Nation!"

After Super Bowl XI, Davis was contemplative in a way that one might imagine Ike was after accepting surrender in the Rheims schoolhouse, or Lincoln when told Lee had not put up a fuss at Appomattox. Madden was more relieved than anything else. Stabler, Matuszak, Biletnikoff, and the other wildmen that made up this team knew that, just as in the Grand Funk Railroad classic, "Now, these fine ladies, they had a plan..." they were out to become the embodiment of those desires!

But Davis could not outwardly enjoy it. Like Ike and Lincoln, like Patton who had seen too much war, Davis had seen too much disappointment. He sat in the Rose Bowl's luxury box. Well-wishers began to hover around him, offering their congratulations. Davis never moved from his chair, staring at the field of play. There was no joy in his eyes. He seemed to have achieved revenge more than victory.

"HOLY ROLLER"

In 1978, Oakland trailed San Diego 20–14 with the ball at the Charger 15, with mere seconds left, and no time outs. With the Raiders receivers covered, Woody Lowe hit Ken Stabler. Instead of going down for the count, he "fumbled" the ball forward in the desperate hope that it would bounce enough yards for a first down and be recovered by the Raiders. With the clock winding down to nothing, the ball did bounce crazily forward. Pete Banaszak "pushed" it at the 3. Dave Casper fell on it for the winning touchdown, 21–20. Bill King's call of this play is considered one of the greatest in broadcast history, in which he gets existential—"is anything real anymore"—and comical. "Madden wants to know if it's real. The referee says yes, get yer big butt out of here. He does." The NFL declared, "There shalt be no more 'Holy Rollers,'" however, changing the rules to disallow the forward progress of fumbles.

"I still have the NFL-AFL feeling," he said. "I grew up with it. I remember the obstacles put in our way."

Interestingly, the team they had beaten, Minnesota, was supposed to have been awarded the AFL franchise in 1960. But when the NFL decided to expand, Minnesota opted to go with the established league instead, giving birth to Oakland, the AFL's stepchild.

"Without Al Davis," wrote Jim Murray in the *Los Angeles Times*, "Oakland would be Tampa Bay."

Davis was all about the pursuit, the commitment to excellence. It was as if the actual achievement of it created a weakness, as if only the hunger and desire that emanates from bitter defeat gives a team the real impetus to pay the ultimate price necessary.

Years later, USC football coach Pete Carroll would win consecutive national championships, while talk show host Jim Rome said, "I don't see any reason why he can't win five or 10, like John Wooden." Carroll embraced the attention, the hype, the Heismans, and smilingly told whoever was listening that he just wanted to "keep this going as long as we can."

Carroll's sunny attitude was the total opposite of Al Davis's dismal "I can't be happy" approach. Perhaps this was a Davis flaw, for the Raiders of 1967–1985 were consistently one of the most talented, dominant teams in the game, yet the three Super Bowls won during that span of time are a strange underachievement. They could have, should have won more, perhaps quite a few more.

Nobody maintained excellence as long as they did, though. The Dallas Cowboys were the closest, winning two Super Bowls during a run that stretched from 1966 to 1981, in which they contended and made the playoffs almost every season. The 49ers from 1981 to 1997 fall a couple years short. Lombardi's Packers were a team of the 1960s, but not beyond that.

The Jets, the Colts, the Chiefs, the Dolphins, even the Steelers—they all came and went. Pittsburgh won four Super Bowls, but their ultimate run was really a seven-year stretch compared to what Oakland (and L.A.) did in nearly two decades. But Pittsburgh won the "big one" over and over.

From Davis's perspective, 1976–1977 seemed to be a self-fulfilling prophecy. The Holy Grail had been won. What next? Obviously, the Raiders came back with the goal of winning it, but if Davis was going to "relax"—and loosen his team up by virtue of it—thus giving them the freedom to pursue a second straight title absent the pressures of yesteryear, well, that was not his style.

The Raiders continued to draft well, bringing in defensive backs Mike Davis from Colorado and Lester Hayes from Texas A&M. With Tatum, Atkinson, Brown, Thomas, and Neal Colzie firmly established, they were not going to break into the starting lineup soon but would certainly pay dividends down the line.

Rod Martin was a 12th-round selection from USC, overlooked by the rest of the league but chosen by Davis based on John McKay's strong recommendation. Aside from rookies Mickey Marvin, Randy McClanahan, and Jeff Barnes, tackle Mike McCoy and end Pat Toomay were brought in. When the season started, Oakland looked better than ever in a 24–0 pasting of San Diego, in which Charger quarterback James Harris was held to 77 yards passing.

Terry Bradshaw could not get Pittsburgh moving in the Raiders' 16–7 win over the Steelers. At that point, it certainly appeared that, in the Patton-versus-Rommel struggle for supremacy between these two franchises, the Silver and Black had gained the upper hand.

Trailing Kansas City 21–10, Oakland rallied behind Davis's 37-yard touchdown run. When Cleveland went down 26–10, the Raiders were 4–0 for the first time. Maybe they would have been better off dealing with their usual adversity—an upset loss in the opener, perhaps. It was too smooth, at least until Denver came to town.

Since the creation of the American Football League, the Broncos were an underperforming team playing in a cowtown. The Raiders did not even consider them a rival, really, just another division foe to get fat on. But in 1977, that all turned around, with a thud. The Broncos were doing it with defense, winning by scores like 7–0, which was not particularly impressive to anybody, least of all the Raiders and their "fireworks and fury" offense.

Quarterback Craig Morton was a San Jose guy and an All-American at Cal. A hard partier, he was one of those guys who found spirituality, turning his life around for the better. But as a QB, he was yesterday's news. He never filled Don Meredith's shoes at Dallas and eventually lost his job to Roger Staubach. Many people did not even know he was still in football when he brought the unbeaten Broncos to the Coliseum, but they all knew about it after he engineered the 30–7 beat-down of the defending world champions of professional football.

Knowing the ride back to the Super Bowl might be bumpy, Oakland got serious, prevailing over Richard Todd and the Jets 28–27. Only two weeks after losing to them, they faced the Broncos again, on a Monday night at Mile High Stadium. The Raiders decided to demonstrate they were not over the hill just yet, led by Toomay sacking the slow-footed Morton four times in a 24–14 win.

"It was a hell of a victory," said Madden.

Wins over Seattle and Houston had Oakland on a roll, but another old punching bag, the Chargers, asserted themselves in a 12–7 win, their first against the Raiders since 1968.

Pro football is not like college. The vagaries of a long season wear a team down. Maintaining the mental edge is hard. Each team is composed of fellow pros. The talent differential in the NFL is not nearly as great as it is in the collegiate game, where a Tennessee is virtually an automatic over a Vanderbilt, an Ohio State usually a sure thing against a Miami of Ohio.

With the playoff system, of course, each game is not as important as a college schedule in which an unbeaten season is often necessary in order to finish number one. Some would say that gambling influences can make the pro football bounce in funny ways, too.

TOP 10

Raider Rivalries

1. Denver Broncos
2. Pittsburgh Steelers
3. Kansas City Chiefs
4. San Diego Chargers
5. Miami Dolphins
6. New England Patriots
7. New York Jets
8. San Francisco 49ers
9. Cleveland Browns
10. Washington Redskins

So it was with the 1977 Raiders, who got stretched toward the end. After suffering ignominious defeat at the hands of the normally lowly Chargers, they beat Buffalo, only to lose to the Rams in L.A., 20–14. Denver, full of vim and vinegar, stayed strong throughout and won the West with a 12–2 mark versus Oakland's 11–3. The wild-card berth it brought them was, by their high standards, a letdown.

Forced to travel, which in January, of course, means cool weather, Oakland found themselves surrounded by 60,763 Baltimore fans screaming for blood. In a true classic, Stabler dueled Colt quarterback Bert Jones, the lead changing hands in the manner of the Miami-Oakland classic of 1974. Stabler liked going to Casper in this game, but the Oakland defense could not contain the gunslinging LSU product, Jones.

Needing three to tie, Snake engineered one of those patented drives that are remembered so well, nailing the big tight end on the classic "ghost to the post" play for 42 yards. Then Madden played it close to the vest, settling for Errol Mann's 22-yard field goal to send the 31-all game into overtime.

Both teams stalled until the second OT, when Snake found Cliff Branch for 19 yards, setting up Casper in the end zone to send the 37–31 winners into Denver for a game that, in their minds, would truly separate the contenders from the pretenders.

The fact that Denver manhandled a fine Pittsburgh club to get to the title game should have been all the caution they needed. Playing in front of the legendary Denver crazies in winter cold, there was no way Oakland could legitimately expect to dictate and dominate.

In the end they should have won, but Rob Lytle's fumble and subsequent recovery by Mike McCoy was not seen by the referee, giving Denver another shot at the goal line, which they converted—enough to give them a 20–17 victory that goes down in the pantheon of Raider disappointments.

"What's going on here?" Davis yelled from the press box, where he saw the play with his own eyes and on the TV monitors, which do not lie. "That's a fumble."

After the game, instead of admitting their mistakes, the referees defended the bad call, causing Davis to compare it to Vietnam.

"The Big Lie," he called it.

Jack Tatum began a long tradition that some call excuses, but others say is right on. He stated that the referees were prejudiced against Oakland because of the "criminal element" and Davis's strident feud with Rozelle.

THE UGLY

"THE IMMACULATE RECEPTION"

Only true historians know about the infamous "Merkle's Boner," in which Fred Merkle's failure to touch second base led to an improbable replay of a 1908 game between the New York Giants and Chicago Cubs, costing New York the National League pennant.

Brooklyn Dodger fans of course live with the memory of Bobby Thomson's "Shot Heard 'Round the World" in 1951. The Boston Red Sox can choose from a buffet of failure, highlighted by Johnny Pesky holding the ball (1946) and Bill Buckner's bent frame while an easy grounder skipped underneath his glove (1986).

In the entire history of sports, however, there are two losses more bitter to swallow than any others. Both occurred within a few months of each other in 1972. In September, the U.S. Olympic basketball team had the gold medal literally, absolutely, and beyond all question stolen from them by corrupt Communist officials in the star-crossed Munich Games.

In December, the Oakland Raiders lost "the Immaculate Reception" AFC playoff game to Pittsburgh. The two abominable defeats—the American hoopsters and the Raider gridders—were different in character. The Olympic debacle, of course, was a national disaster, cheered in this country by nobody.

The Raider loss to Pittsburgh was a "horse of a different color."

Gloom in Oakland was matched by joy in Pittsburgh. The Raiders, even though they had not yet won any Super Bowls, were already considered an "Evil Empire" of sorts five years before *Star Wars* came out. Their pain was met with a certain amount of glee, and while Raider diehards take the time-honored stance that the call against them was a bad one, it is not nearly as cut and dried as the Munich heist.

For Raider fans of a certain age, they all remember where they were when Franco Harris ran to glory, amidst great confusion, joy, and despair. The play resembled "the Play," when Cal ran through the Stanford band to win the 1982 Big Game. "The Play" involved a certain amount of skill, mixed with luck. "The Immaculate Reception" was so fluky as to almost discount the skill of Harris in being where he was, alertly reacting to what was happening, catching the ball and running like the wind.

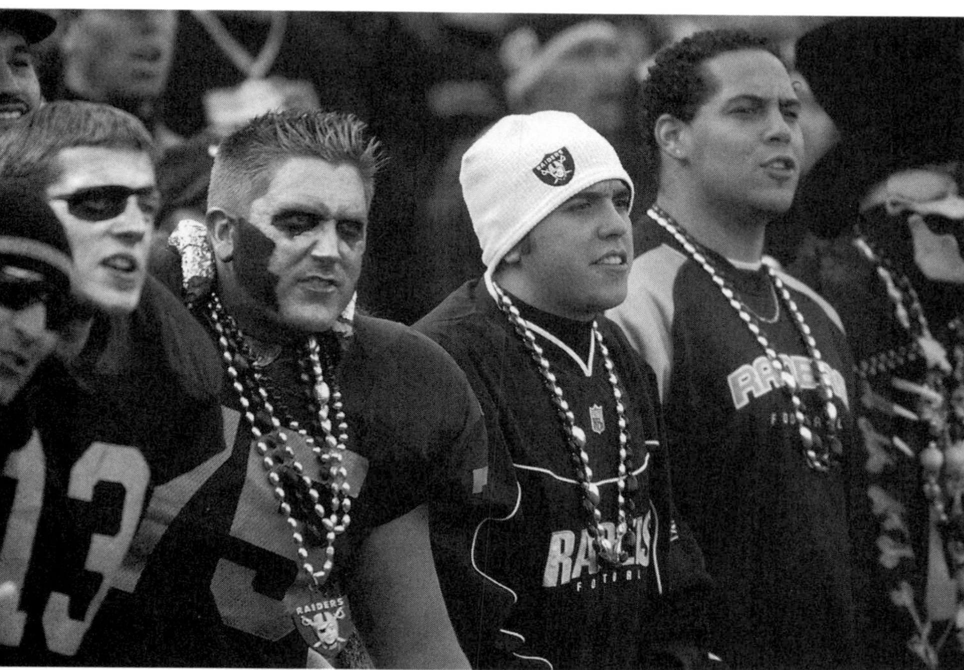

Raiders fans perfectly reflect their team—they are among the rowdiest and most rabid in the NFL and heartily embrace the franchise's outlaw image as cultivated by owner Al Davis.

WHEN THE FAT LADY SINGS

In his autobiography, *Snake*, Ken Stabler wrote of "the Immaculate Reception": "I decided that for me to run 30 yards for a touchdown against the Steeler defense was a miracle, so I guessed Pittsburgh deserved one, too."

An examination of the rules and circumstances of "the Immaculate Reception," murky or not, leave the Raiders swallowing the same bitter "we've been robbed" pill to swallow as the 1972 Olympic basketball team. Both of the disastrous events are replayed regularly on ESPN Classic. The fact that the Olympic call was illegally upheld is made apparent every time, but the Raider-Steeler vantage point more resembles Republicans and Democrats squabbling. What never changes is that queasy feeling, like watching JFK's motorcade turn down Dealey Plaza. Uneasiness somehow pervades the senses. *This time* it won't happen, but it inevitably bears the same unbearable result.

After the crazy 1970 season, in which Oakland trailed 20–17 late in the AFC title game at Baltimore before falling short by 10, the team experienced a disappointing 1971 campaign. Kansas City regained the Western Division before losing in an extraordinary double overtime game to the ascending Miami Dolphins. Dallas finally won their "big one" when Roger Staubach directed the Cowboys to a resounding victory over Miami, but Don Shula's team was loaded in 1972. They went undefeated in the regular season, the only club to have done that until the 2007 New England Patriots matched the feat.

Coach John Madden began to separate himself from Al Davis, calling more and more of his own plays. Early on, he gave Ken Stabler his opportunity to play, but the experiment did not take. Lamonica was reinstated and put together another fine season, leading the Raiders to a 10–3–1 regular-season record.

Pittsburgh finally made the postseason for the first time in their history. Owner Art Rooney's team had moved into Three Rivers Stadium, a shiny all-purpose facility with artificial turf.

TOP 10

Game-Changing Bad Calls of All-Time

1. U.S.-U.S.S.R. Olympic basketball game, 1972: extra time gives Soviets victory.
2. Cardinals-Royals, 1985 World Series: Don Denkinger's missed call denies Card win.
3. Colorado-Missouri, 1990: Fifth down elevates Buffaloes to "national championship."
4. **Raiders-Steelers, 1972: "Immaculate Reception" called when officials learn of lack of security.**
5. Yankees-Orioles, 1996 playoffs: Fan interference not called on Derek Jeter homer.
6. **Raiders-Broncos, 1977: Rob Lytle's fumble not called in Denver win.**
7. Argentina-England, 1986 World Cup: Maradona's "hand of God" goal.
8. **Raiders-Patriots, 2002 playoffs: Tom Brady's fumble not called in Pats' win.**
9. Steelers-Lions, 1998: Jerome Bettis's "tails" call is heard as "heads" and Lions win.
10. Stars-Sabres, 1999 Stanley Cup: Brett Hull's skate in the crease gives the Stars the win.

Terry Bradshaw, the first pick of the 1970 Draft, came into his own. They were loaded with young talent and were evenly matched with Oakland.

Entering the playoffs, Miami's unbeaten year would have to survive that hobgoblin of greatness, the law of averages. The feeling was that if the Dolphins could be beaten, Oakland was just the team to do it, but they had to get past the upstart Steelers, who just a few years earlier under coach Chuck Noll had finished 1–13.

The Steel City is football-crazy. Western Pennsylvania is renowned for producing great quarterbacks: Johnny Unitas, Jim Kelly, Dan Marino, Joe Montana, just to highlight a few. *Finally,* the Steelers were giving them something to cheer about, but there was none of the sunny optimism of the California sports aficionado. Steeler fans had the same dread in their hearts as long-suffering Red Sox and Cub supporters.

It was December, a sunny, hard day on the unforgiving plastic turf. Lamonica was given the start, but it was another big-game disappointment for Daryle. Bradshaw, despite all the offensive weapons at his disposal, was not much better, but two Roy Gerela field goals gave Pittsburgh a perilous 6–0 lead. Steeler fans could see disaster hovering over Three Rivers Stadium like the *Hindenburg*.

"When you get into these things with the Oakland Raiders, you start to worry," said Noll. "They've been involved in these wild finishes so often that they almost take them for granted. These sorts of things would tear the nervous systems right out of most athletes."

Blood dotted the turf, much of it Lamonica's. Four of his passes were smashed back in his face, the ultimate form of bad feedback, by L.C. Greenwood, "Mean Joe" Greene, Ben McGee, and Dwight White.

Marv Hubbard got the call out of the Oakland backfield, taking great punishment. Steeler fans, bundled in the late afternoon shadows, their breath filling the air like the nearby smoke stacks, knew too well the Raider penchant for late-game heroics. George Blanda was still very much in play. They had hope, but girded themselves for disappointment, too. Their desperate shouts filled the winter air, more pleas than encouragement.

It was not Blanda, however, whom Madden went to in a pinch. Off the bench came a long-haired southpaw, Ken Stabler. Stabler had delivered victory out of the jaws of defeat for Bear Bryant at Alabama, where he replaced Joe Namath, leading 'Bama to an unbeaten season in 1966 before Davis selected him. However, he was not a sure thing. Whereas Lamonica was the prototypical strong-armed NFL quarterback, Stabler did not have that kind of strength. He was a renegade, a problem child, a wild partier, but maybe that "devil may care" attitude was what was needed in replacing Lamonica, who seemingly was wound so

BY THE NUMBERS

270 (pounds)—The average weight of a Raider offensive lineman in the early-to-mid 1970s.

tight a pin could not be pulled from his rear with a tractor.

Stabler had three minutes left to work magic, and he proved to be Houdini in that gloaming. It took a dozen plays, but Stabler had Oakland down to the Pittsburgh 30 when he rolled out, was flushed from the pocket, and did what Lamonica could never do. He scrambled, found the sideline, and ran untouched into the end zone. After Blanda's extra point, Pittsburghers just stared at each other, mocked by the scoreboard, their own knowledge of fate, and inevitable defeat.

On the Oakland sideline, Madden's men rejoiced, beginning to think about Miami. With 1:13 to go, however, Bradshaw had life. He moved Pittsburgh 20 yards to their own 40-yard line, but then the great Jack Tatum took over. He knocked down two passes, then barely missed an interception. Twenty-two seconds left. Fourth-and-10. Bradshaw had no time for anything except a desperate bomb to Frenchy Fuqua, running a curl pattern.

Tatum and Fuqua collided like two freight trains. The ball hit them, bouncing violently off their shoulder pads. Whether the ball hit Tatum or Fuqua—thus determining whether the call was bad or not—is still hard to determine. If it hit off Fuqua, it was dead to the Steelers, since no offensive players could catch a ball that hit a teammate first.

Tatum was receiving slaps and congratulations on the game-winning play when everybody noticed, to their horror, that running back Franco Harris—an All-American out of Penn State and a star who had been totally bottled up all day—alertly caught the deflected pass inches before it hit the turf. He was off and running. There was no time left. All the Raiders needed to do was *stop him.*

It was not to be. Harris raced into the end zone. Delirium ensued. Howls of protests erupted on the Raider sideline. Confusion reigned, and Pittsburgh fans knew full well that any number of scenarios or technicalities could erase the play, which in the scheme of their sorry history seemed almost to be written by the hand of God.

Madden argued that the ball hit Fuqua first, making it a dead play. There was no instant replay, but even if there had been it would have been inconclusive. Referee Fred Swearingen tentatively signaled that Tatum, not Fuqua, had touched the ball, which meant the play would stand, but he was simply guessing!

He left the field and ran into the baseball dugout to find a phone, where he placed a call to Art McNally, the supervisor of NFL officials. Did Swearingen want to know what the replay showed?

"He asked one question," recalled Madden. "He asked how many cops there were at Three Rivers Stadium to protect him if he reversed the call."

Apparently, not enough.

Swearingen emerged and raised his hands: "Touchdown!"

The newspaper photos apparently showed what the film did not, that Fuqua had touched it, making it a dead ball, but it did not matter. Pittsburgh 13, Oakland 7.

PAIN AND SUFFERING

1967: Lost to Green Bay in the Super Bowl
1968: Lost to "Broadway Joe" Namath and the "Super Jets"
1969: Lost to Kansas City in the AFL title game
1972: Lost to Pittsburgh in the "Immaculate Reception" game
1974: Lost to underdog Steelers at home in AFC Championship Game
1975: Lost to Steelers on an icy Three Rivers Stadium in AFC title game
1977: Lost to Denver when Rob Lytle's fumble was not called
1991: Smoked in the snow at Buffalo in AFC title game
2001: Baltimore's defense overwhelms Raiders in AFC title game
2002: The "Brady tuck" fumble is not called, Pats win AFC
2003: Barret Robbins goes AWOL, Gruden gets Tampa "Super revenge"

"That's the way it will have to go into the record books, because that's what the officials said happened," philosophized Davis. "We'll just have to find our pride and poise again in 1973. What else is there to do? One of the worst things that can happen to a football team is to make excuses then sit around believing them. The Oakland Raiders will not let that happen."

HUNTER THOMPSON, THE HELL'S ANGELS, AND THE CRIMINAL ELEMENT

The Oakland Raiders have a dark image. Defensive stars George Atkinson and Jack Tatum were among the Raiders who some said were "dirty players." Tatum's hit of New England's Darryl Stingley, which resulted in Stingley's paralysis, played a big role in that reputation. Atkinson had his share of on-field run-ins with Pittsburgh and other teams. Later Raider ruffians like John Matuszak and Lyle Alzado played the outlaw image to the hilt. Al Davis was no small reason for the "criminal" moniker. He wanted to be feared, like a mob boss from his native Brooklyn. The team colors suggested just such a thing. The Raiders were hated and feared by the Chiefs, Chargers, Steelers, Jets, Dolphins...

But the image of the outlaw Raiders was solidified by an outlaw "gonzo journalist," Dr. Hunter S. Thompson, also known as Raoul Duke. Thompson was not, just in case the gentle reader is unaware, an actual "doctor" of anything. Thompson, a native of Kentucky, wrote blistering, drug- and alcohol-induced, anti-establishment screeds of such brilliant wit and humor as to engender the grudging admiration of those he savaged.

Thompson actually served in the Air Force, which consisted of his driving his commanders out of their minds while writing for the Air Force newspaper—when not AWOL, that is.

In the mid-1960s, Thompson made his name when he walked straight into the brutal world of the Oakland, California–based Hell's Angels. The Angels thought him a sissified scribe until Thompson demonstrated his ability to out-drink, out-drug, and out-anything else the Angels did. It established his bona fides as a national writer of substance just as America was changing. It also gave him Bay Area imprimatur, enhanced by subsequent assignments from the then San Francisco–based *Rolling Stone* magazine.

In the early 1970s, Thompson became a legend of the written word with his magnum opus, *Fear and Loathing in Las Vegas*, a book so brilliant, yet so crude, as to be beyond the ability to translate. He followed it up with a scathing look at politics, exposing the art form of electioneering as an open, bleeding sore called *Fear and Loathing on the Campaign Trail '72*.

By 1973, Thompson was not a writer—he was a cult—his readers as loyal as those of Ernest Hemingway's or F. Scott Fitzgerald's were in their day. An enormous sports fan and inveterate gambler, Thompson set his sights on the cult of personality that by then was Al Davis. His pal was Dave Burgin, this author's editor with *The* (San Francisco) *Examiner* 28 years after the events of this story. Burgin is a man known as the "Billy Martin of sports editors" because he would take over a failing paper, turn it around, then wear out his welcome. Burgin told Thompson that Davis and the Raiders (along with Pittsburgh) were "the only two teams in the whole league flaky enough" for Thompson to "identify" with.

Davis may have read books about military generals, but only to glean what he could for football knowledge. He did not have the slightest idea who Dr. Hunter Thompson was. He had never heard of *Rolling Stone*.

DRUG STORE

Dr. Hunter S. Thompson *supposedly* did a mind-boggling amount of narcotic drugs, *supposedly* conducted interviews with a number of Raiders in a seedy Oakland biker bar, and *supposedly* did one of his most famous interviews in relation to—sort of—a football game. In his classically biting tome *Fear and Loathing On the Campaign Trail '72*, a book filled with fantastic stories of "facts" weaved in mesmerizing yet fanciful detail around people and events—what is true or not is murky to this day—Thompson claimed that, during the week of the 1973 Super Bowl between Miami and Washington, he scored an interview with President Richard Nixon under the *proviso* that the subject be limited to football!

ON THE ROAD

A few years after the release of *Easy Rider*, Raider behemoths Ben Davidson and Tom Keating took a motorcycle trip to Mexico which, according to legend, matched Dr. Hunter S. Thompson's famed 1971 trip to Las Vegas to cover a dirt bike race.

"Who's the guy over there with the ball in his hand?" Davis asked when he saw the stoned-looking Thompson infiltrating one of his super-secret practice sessions.

"His name's Thompson," said *San Francisco Chronicle* sportswriter Jack Smith, who apparently had been cleared for entry into the inner sanctum. Smith added that Thompson was from *Rolling Stone*.

"The Rolling Stones?" Davis ejaculated. "Jesus Christ! What's he *doing* here? Did *you* bring him?"

"No, he's writing a big article," said Smith. "*Rolling Stone* is a magazine, Al. It's different from the Rolling Stones; they're a rock music group....Thompson's a buddy of George Plimpton's, I think...and he's also a friend of Dave Burgin's—you remember Burgin?"

"Holy s**t! Burgin!" Davis practically vomited his name. "We ran him out of here with a cattle prod!"

Smith explained that Thompson had written "a good book about Las Vegas." Of course, if Davis had read Thompson's descriptions of *A Savage Journey to the Heart of the American Dream*, he would have arranged for Thompson to be burned at the stake on the 50-yard line.

Thompson observed that Davis looked like "a pimp or a track-tout."

"Get the bastard out of here. I don't trust him," was Davis's assessment of Thompson, the author of the "good book about Las Vegas."

Thompson described his experience "covering" Davis's Raiders as "massive slander," mixed with "a series of personal professional

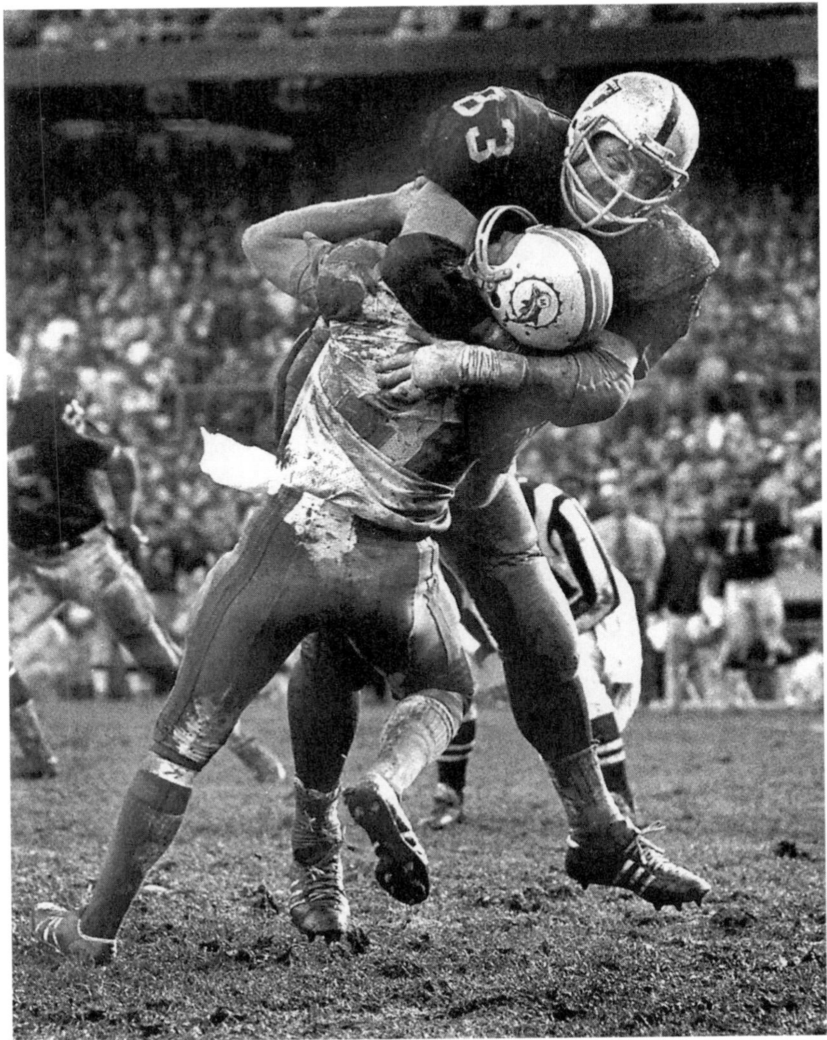

Raiders defensive end, "Big Ben" Davidson—all 6′8″ of him—has a stranglehold on Dolphins quarterback Bob Griese. After football, Davidson went on to a modestly successful career as an actor.

disasters...a beating by stadium cops outside the Raider dressing room," and, of course, "total banishment" from "the field, locker room, press box...bar, restaurant, zoo, or shotgun store" where any Raiders might be found.

Because of their aggressive style and in-your-face attitude, playing the Raiders was never an easy task. Here a gang of Oakland tacklers raises a cloud of dust as they wrap up a Colts ball carrier.

He also described Davis, aside from looking like a "track-tout," as "a small wiry man in a tan golf jacket with a greasy duck-tail haircut who paced along the sideline on both fields with a speedy kind of intensity," all of which caused Thompson "bad vibes" from Davis's "fiendish intensity of...speech and mannerisms," which Hunter then said were strongly reminiscent of "another Oakland badass," the focus of his book on the Hell's Angels. That was the gang's "president," the infamous Ralph "Sonny" Barger, who had recently beat a multiple-murder rap, along with assorted charges of heroin possession with intent to sell, weapons, sexual assault on minors, intent to commit forcible sodomy, and God knows what other pleasantries.

Somehow, by hook or crook, Thompson did manage to get close enough to his subject to fashion an astounding piece, even getting Davis to talk at length about "Environmental Determinism." Apparently, Davis tried to buy property in Aspen, Colorado (where Thompson lived), but was rebuffed because his money was "dirty" and he had "connections in Las Vegas."

Dr. Hunter S. Thompson's dramatizations of Al Davis sounded much like that of a journalistic depiction of Pontius Pilate's hand-washing during the trial of Christ. A writer specializing in verbal savagery scaled the heights of his art in painting this Davis portrait.

Thus, with the publication in one of *Rolling Stone*'s best-selling editions at the height of the magazine's success, by its most popular and infamous writer, was the Raider "criminal element" image born.

"Any society that will put Barger in jail and make Al Davis a respectable millionaire at the same time is not a society to be trifled with," remarked Thompson, as if warning the locals of the consequences of going to war with Rome.

Aside from having written the "good book about Las Vegas," Thompson had run for sheriff of Aspen, causing the establishment of Aspen to come *this close* to hiring some "Las Vegas connections" to end his candidacy with extreme prejudice. This serendipity was just enough to allow Thompson slight access to Davis, which was like getting an up-close-and-personal with Mephistopheles.

Somehow, Davis and Thompson bonded, ever so slightly and for just a short period of time, but Thompson got as close to Davis as anybody, which is not saying much. Davis *almost* accepted an invitation to meet the good doctor in a local tavern, then suddenly turned to Thompson and asked, "What are you after? Why are you here?"

Thompson never did have that beer with the owner, but he did quaff a few with Raider players, which was certainly not a hard rendezvous to make. They were all amazed that he even got within five feet of Davis.

"The world really is changing when you see a thing like that—Hunter Thompson and Al Davis [standing side by side in broad daylight]," one player was quoted.

The *Rolling Stone* article, later reprinted as "*Mano a Mano* with the Oakland Raiders" in Thompson's book *The Great Shark Hunt*, was as masterful as all his other work. Davis probably ordered his underlings to scour America, buy every copy, and burn it, but it actually worked to his advantage. It was more fodder for the mystique of Davis and his team, who he wanted to be feared...and loathed.

THE ASSASSIN

There is a scene toward the end of Francis Ford Coppola's *Apocalypse Now* in which Marlon Brando, playing Colonel Walter Kurtz, addresses Martin Sheen, the bedeviled Special Forces hit man assigned to kill him.

"Are you an assassin?" Kurtz mocks Willard.

"I'm a soldier," says Willard.

"You're neither," boasts Kurtz. "You're an errand boy, sent by grocery clerks, to collect the bill."

The Raiders' "assassin," Jack Tatum, was no "errand boy," but he collected many a "bill," in the form of enemies felled by his "bullets." Unfortunately, Tatum's reputation is tarnished by the fact that he laid a wicked hit on New England's Darryl Stingley, which paralyzed Stingley for life. Tatum reportedly never visited Stingley or expressed any real remorse.

Tatum was not a lovable character. There is little evidence that there is anything to admire about him, with the exception of his considerable football skills. Not everybody can be Ronnie Lott. Tatum was dangerous, a man who "looks out at the world through narrow slits," wrote Wells Twombly of *The* (San Francisco) *Examiner*. It is interesting that Tatum is viewed as he is, in part because of the way he hit. Lott did the same thing, but through God's grace nobody was ever sent to life in a wheelchair by virtue of it.

TOP 10

All-Time Greatest Defensive Backs

1. **Ronnie Lott**
2. Rod Woodson
3. Herb Adderley
4. Night Train Lane
5. Mel Blount
6. Deion Sanders
7. **Willie Brown**
8. Mel Renfro
9. **Mike Haynes**
10. Willie Wood-*t*
    Jimmy Johnson-*t*
    Jack Tatum-*t*

Had Tatum had a more engaging personality, he might have received a little bit of leeway from his critics, but like Barry Bonds he had no reserves of goodwill from which to draw. He was just piled on, as happened with Bonds after it was discovered that he was juiced to the gills.

Perhaps it can be said that Tatum had a "little man's complex." Memory somehow paints the portrait of a big hulk, a power force laying thunder sticks on unsuspecting ball carriers, but in reality he was only 5′10″, weighing in at a paltry 205 pounds.

Somehow, Tatum's demeanor, his stare, his Afro—*something* about the man made him look bigger than he was. Many who do not know pro football very well assume he was a linebacker, or even a lineman, not a defensive back, whose main job is more speed-related than tackle-related. After all, "Neon Deion" Sanders was an All-Pro playing in the secondary, where he broke up passes but avoided tackling people as if they were covered with bubonic plague.

Tatum came out of Woody Hayes's program at Ohio State. Hayes was a progressive who built the Buckeyes into greatness recruiting terrific black players like Tatum. Tatum was a prep

Lester Hayes' hands reveal the coating of stickum that he always generously applied—which led to the league banning the substance. The aggressive cornerback earned a spot in the NFL Hall of Fame after starring for the Raiders from 1977 to 1986.

fullback. Hayes loved his aggressiveness and saw him as a blitzing safety who could stop the run and the pass.

In 1968, the sophomore-laden Buckeyes went unbeaten, defeating the star-laden USC Trojans and O.J. Simpson in the Rose Bowl for the national championship. In 1969, *Sports Illustrated* boldly stated that the Bucks were the greatest collegiate football team of all time, but they were upset by Michigan 24–12. In 1970, Tatum, Rex Kern, and the rest of Hayes's Buckeyes were seniors. Again, they smashed through the Big 10 unbeaten and untied. Effete Stanford was their last obstacle in the Rose Bowl, but Heisman Trophy–winning quarterback Jim Plunkett led the Indians (as they were known back then) to one of the greatest upsets ever recorded, 27–17, and the biggest victory in Stanford sports history.

Hayes had a conniption fit every time he brought his teams to the West Coast. He told his charges that "people out here aren't rooting for you," directing them to just be polite. Woody failed to heed his own words, going so far as to throw a punch at an *L.A. Times* photographer. Tatum seemed to inherit Hayes's "chip on the shoulder" attitude.

A few years after Tatum, Ohio State featured a superstar defensive back named Neal Colzie, who tended to mouth off and create histrionics on the field. He, too, was burned by a Pac-8 team, USC, in the 1975 Rose Bowl, before he joined Tatum on the Raiders.

TRIVIA

When did Al Davis assume sole control of the Raider franchise?

Find the answers on page 177.

"This is the meanest tackler I ever coached," Hayes once said of Tatum. "I understand that once Jack has hit you, you never forget him."

Al Davis liked that kind of attitude. He wanted to be feared more than respected, and certainly not loved. That was Tatum's style all the way. After being drafted in the first round by Oakland—in his case, there was no hiding him, the Silver and Black were fortunate he was still around—he walked into training camp and assumed dominance. There was no deferring to the veterans, the coach, the team's history. In his mind, he was the new starting safety, and he was. Self-confidence oozed from his every pore.

"I always knew I could play in the pros," he stated. "I'm not stupid, though. I know I can learn a lot. I knew from the beginning that I would be a starter for the Raiders. This is my kind of football team—no nonsense, all business. I like that. When I was in high school, you had to be tough or you got killed playing football. There's nothing funny about this game."

As a rookie, Tatum told one veteran player, "I know you guys aren't interested in rookies who have big names and don't deliver. Well, I'm one rookie who can help you *now*."

Tatum teamed with Phil Villapiano and it proved to be one of the keys to pushing the team into uncharted territory. Tatum's success coincided with the creation of a more complete team. It was all part of the Raiders' ability to keep up with growing trends in the game. The Raiders of the pre-Tatum era were a "bombs away" offensive juggernaut that definitely placed more emphasis on scoring than defense. But as the merger was completed in 1970, defensive coordinators and rules changes regarding the old AFL "bump 'n' run" were modified. The wide-open passing schemes of the Sid Gillman era were replaced by the defensive genius of coaches like Tom Landry and Chuck Noll.

The size of the players increased. The "hybrid" linebacker would come into existence, just as the pass-catching tight end made that skill necessary. Blitz packages required great speed and athleticism, which was Tatum's forte. Tatum is regarded as an all-time great Raider and certainly an NFL legend. The Stingley episode hurt him, and he is not in the Hall of Fame, but those who competed against Jack would state he was as nasty and difficult to play against as any safety in history. It may take a while, but Jack will someday accept induction to the Hall of Fame in his native Ohio.

IN THE CLUTCH

1963–1965: SAVING THE OAKLAND FRANCHISE

Part of the Al Davis strategy was to take advantage of the fact that he and his team were underestimated. Davis had played that hand all his life, using the power of low expectations to sneak up on opponents—often using evasion, trickery, and deception in the manner of Joseph Stalin, Franklin Roosevelt, and Mao Tse-tung (just to name three people he personally mentioned as models for this tactic). Then, once gaining the upper hand, he replaced that with fear and intimidation to consolidate his gains.

Oakland was the perfect staging ground for such a strategy. They were the anti-California of the Beach Boys '60s. Los Angeles was Hollywood—glamour, the surf life, beautiful girls. Orange County represented wealth and political power. San Diego was the good life. San Francisco was elegance and Old World style.

Oakland made Cincinnati look like a world capital. When teams arrived in Oakland, every sight and sound lulled them into downgrading their opponent. The airport was chintzy, the hotel was rickety, the restaurants cheap, the bars were dives, the women were unattractive, the men still stuck in the Great Depression. Once at Youell Field, the "stadium" suffered in comparison with the sports monuments of New York, L.A., and Boston. The fans were provincial.

Then the contest would start, and it was a whole new ballgame. Davis would advertise himself as the father of the

BEHIND THE SCENES

Mr. Ed Bercovich ran a furniture store (and maybe a few other things). He is a close, personal friend of Raiders owner Al Davis. Whenever talk would break out about new stadium financing, or a reshuffling of the ownership group, Bercovich's name would pop up. You never saw his picture. He was not a media dude, but he was a mover and a shaker. Maybe he owned some land or had some parking lots that could be converted into the Raiders new football palace. He had money, he loved sports, and he was connected to the powers-that-be. He also sponsored the greatest high school summer baseball program in Bay Area history, one that produced superstars like Livermore's Randy Johnson.

wide-open passing game. He surely was an innovator, and Bill Walsh, the West Coast offense impresario who coached under him, called him a genius, but Davis basically copied what he had learned under Sid Gillman.

Copycat or not, give Davis credit for learning well. But there is also no question that he was an innovator in his own right. After the Raiders had gone 6–8 (1960), 2–12 (1961), and 1–13 (1962), rookie coach Davis turned the team around in miraculous fashion. He fashioned the silver-and-black color scheme that remains their trademark to this day. At first it was rejected because when the *Tribune* ran color photos, it was thought they would look like black-and-white, but the image was powerful in person.

In 1963, a little-known quarterback from the San Joaquin Valley by way of the University of the Pacific (a kind of "minor league" for the early Raiders), Tom Flores led the team to a 10–4 mark. Running back Clem Daniels was a star. Center Jim Otto was the best in the business. Receiver Art Powell was a typical example of the Davis type of player.

Powell was an early free agent (the AFL in many ways gave birth to the modern economics of pro sports), having played out his contract with the New York Titans, who bid him, "Good riddance." He was what might be described as a "black agitator." It

Al Davis (shown with Jim Otto, No. 00, on the sideline) demanded complete control of the Raiders when he was hired in 1963—despite his lack of head-coaching experience. He responded by saving the failing franchise and leading it to the top of the AFL.

was felt that he was prejudiced against white people and could not work with them. In Davis, he found a colorblind man who cared only about winning, and in this environment he thrived.

In Davis's first regular-season game, the Raiders shocked the defending Eastern Division champion Houston Oilers, 24–13, on the road. This created enough interest to sell out Youell Field when the Raiders returned home to face Buffalo. That, combined with a resounding 35–17 victory, is credited with propelling the first major political steps toward the building of the Coliseum, completed a mere three years later.

When his players tried to give him the game ball, Davis replied in typical fashion: "I'm not a sentimental guy. I only like to win." Oakland stalled at midseason, which included a disastrous three-

IF ONLY...

The Raiders had not flourished under Al Davis, creating the political will to build the Oakland–Alameda County Coliseum in time for the 1966 season, the city most likely would never have attracted the A's (1968) and later the Warriors, who moved over from San Francisco's Cow Palace when the Coliseum Arena was built in the early 1970s.

game Eastern road trip, but finished the 1963 campaign with eight consecutive wins to close out a successful year. Victories over San Diego on the road and defending champion Kansas City (who captured the '62 AFL crown in Dallas) propelled interest in the team, drawing 600 people to the airport to greet them after beating the Chargers.

The rematch with San Diego at Youell Field exemplified the nascent "pride and poise" label that would resonate with the Davis image. Trailing 27–10, Oakland caused five San Diego turnovers, converting that into a 41–27 win, typical of exciting AFL games.

The season finale was more of the same, further embodying what the league was. The NFL seemed stodgy and boring by comparison. Green Bay under Vince Lombardi had won the 1962 "world championship" by virtue of capturing the NFL playoffs after a 13–1 regular season. They did it the old-fashioned way: defense, a balanced short passing game, and a great running attack led by the Paul Hornung–Jim Taylor combo. In 1963 and 1964, however, the NFL was semi-boring. They were exemplified by the ancient style of George Halas and the Chicago Bears.

DID YOU KNOW...

That in his first year as the Raiders head coach in 1963 Al Davis garnered two awards: AFL Coach of the Year and Oakland's Young Man of the Year?

In that legendary '63 finale at Oakland, Flores and Houston quarterback George Blanda put on a spectacular show. Flores threw for six touchdowns and 407 yards, 247 of them to Powell. The final score:

Raiders 52, Oilers 49. Davis made it clear afterward that he was not through, that his and the team's goal was to establish the "Oakland franchise as a professional football power."

The language of the Raiders' Christmas cards, offering that promise, was all Davis. They did not offer excitement or a winning team. Rather, "power" was the operative word, like Caesar vowing to restore the "glory that was Rome."

Davis was named Coach of the Year, and in a stroke of genius that would embody why his players are so loyal, he deflected all praise toward his players. He was not in it for money, awards, or personal glory. He may not have said it quite like that yet, but he wanted to "just win, baby!"

Over the next two years, Davis further proved what an eye he had for talent. Former USC coach Don Clark told the press that Davis was now "feared" because of this knack for spotting players others missed or were willing to part with, which of course led to embarrassment for the exposed party.

Dan Conners was drafted out of the University of Miami. Ben Davidson was let go by Washington and signed by Oakland. Billy Cannon, the 1959 Heisman Trophy winner whose highly publicized signing by Houston was credited with getting the league off to a good start, was obtained. Davis had his first dispute with Pete Rozelle, who "awarded" Carroll Rosenbloom and Baltimore Arizona State halfback Tony Lorick. In those days, players could be drafted before their college eligibility was over, which caused problems, such as when Davis inked Lorick prior to the NFL Draft. When Baltimore drafted Lorick, a dispute arose, and Rozelle sided with

HALL OF THE VERY GOOD

In 1964, the Raiders signed running back–turned–tight end Billy Cannon. Cannon won the 1959 Heisman Trophy at LSU, and his signing with Houston was considered the first major coup for the AFL. Considered washed up by 1964, he was revitalized by the position change, giving his team star power in their early days.

TRIVIA

How many years did George Blanda play pro football?

Find the answers on page 177.

Rosenbloom, for obvious reasons. Lorick helped the Colts to the 1964 NFL title game; Davis did not forget.

In a loss to Buffalo, Daryle Lamonica, a mostly disappointing reserve quarterback from Notre Dame, led the Bills to a narrow win over Oakland. It did not miss Davis's attention. Davis competed for California's All-American quarterback, Craig Morton. Landing the local hero would be a major coup and a blow to the struggling 49ers. In the end, Dallas outbid the Raiders. Davis later spun the message that he wasn't all that impressed with Morton, and it has been speculated that he did not want the pressure of a "hometown hero" at quarterback because he would be forced to play him. But the message was clear: Davis was a serious contender. It also meant that he needed a quarterback for the future. It would not be Morton. It would be Lamonica.

The 1965 Raiders were 8–5–1, good for second place in the AFL West behind San Diego. The season concluded amid great optimism, centered on the fact that construction of the Coliseum was progressing in time for the team to play there in 1966.

THE MIRACLE WORKER

The opening chapter ("First Period: The Wolf in Winter") of Wells Twombly's biography of George Blanda begins: "Being a description in minute detail of how George Blanda, after only 20 years in professional football, became an overnight sensation."

Indeed, Blanda had toiled in the trenches of professional football since the Truman administration. He was a successful quarterback in the AFL after a less-than-stirring run in the NFL. He was not in the same class as Johnny Unitas, Bart Starr, Joe Namath, or even Daryle Lamonica, but he was a creditable ol' pro.

Blanda is today in the Pro Football Hall of Fame. It is difficult to say, but likely had he not accomplished what he did in 1970, he would not be there. For sure, Blanda was spectacular in

1970, but there was a sense of mysticism about his achievements that season, too. A little bit of luck. Perhaps even miraculous!

Plus, George Blanda owes much of his notoriety to the singular vocal qualities of Mr. Bill King. Those two will be forever, inextricably linked by that season. Like Cosell and Ali, King made Blanda. Blanda made King. In 1970, road games were televised and home games were not. The Raiders sold out every game, but it did not matter. If you did not have a ticket, and if you did not drive 90 miles from Oakland to see the game in a bar or a hotel, then you listened to King on the radio.

There does not seem to be a single adult male who was living in the Bay Area in 1970 who does not vividly recall King announcing, with official succinctness, that "George Blanda is *king of the world!*" after Blanda's field goal beat Cleveland 23–20.

Blanda is something, literally, out of our past. They do not make 'em like that anymore. He is of an era that has come and gone—thankfully—in America: the Great Depression.

Mike Blanda worked deep in the mines. He came home filthy every night but somehow kept his 11 kids from ever knowing they were poor. He taught his children how to compete. Thirteen days after retiring, he passed away, but George was well equipped for whatever life threw his way.

World War II was still going on when Blanda played at Youngwood High School in Pennsylvania. The 6′2″, 215-pound quarterback went to the University of Kentucky, where he played for a fairly famous man: Paul "Bear" Bryant, who is the greatest coach in the history of Kentucky, the greatest coach in the history of Texas A&M, as well as the greatest coach in the history of Alabama...and probably all of collegiate football.

COMEBACK

George Blanda was named American Football Conference Player of the Year in 1970 even though he was not the team's starting quarterback. He came off the bench to lead the team on a string of improbable comebacks.

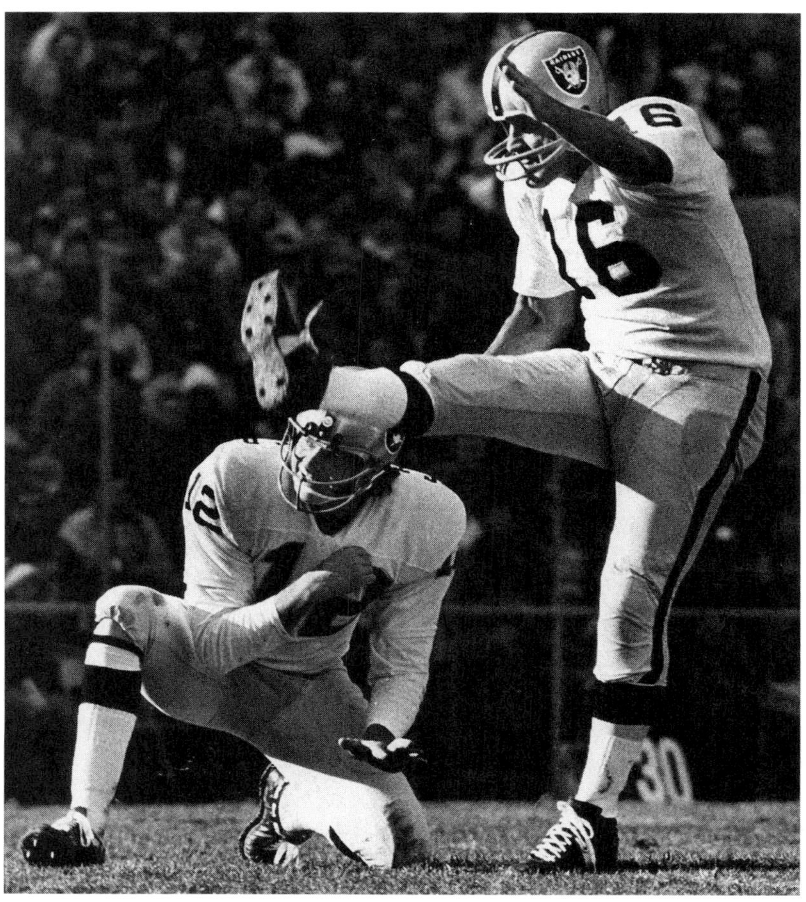

Kicker/quarterback George Blanda was an ageless wonder. Thought washed up numerous times in his 26-season career, Blanda served as an effective backup quarterback into his forties, and was the Raiders kicker until 1976, when he was finally cut by the team at the age of 48.

Blanda started his professional career with the Chicago Bears in 1949. He became one of the top young quarterbacks in the NFL, but fell out of favor with George "Papa Bear" Halas, who "fired" him in 1959.

"I was considered a troublemaker," Blanda recalled. He went to Wrigley Field to "root against the Bears" in 1959, a 32-year-old "washed up" quarterback, but his career was saved by formation of the AFL in 1960.

The Houston Oilers were one of the league's dominant teams in the early years, and Blanda a marquee signal caller. When Pete Beathard of USC came of age, the Oilers decided to go with youth. Blanda's departure marked the franchise's downfall, and there is little evidence that they ever recovered.

He was traded to Oakland in 1967, where he lost a tough quarterback battle with Daryle Lamonica. But Blanda could always punt and kick. With Oakland, he became an integral part of the offense as a place-kicker, knocking 'em in with the old-fashioned straight-foot style.

In 1967, '68, and '69, Blanda kicked field goals and extra points, but he was not entirely happy. He still considered himself a quarterback. But Lamonica's great success was impossible to argue against, so Blanda relegated himself to the backup role.

Controversy swirled around Blanda after the 1969 AFL title game loss to Kansas City. Lamonica injured his hand but was kept in the 17–7 loss despite an inability to move the team in the fourth quarter. Afterward, Blanda was asked if Lamonica should have been removed in favor of him. Blanda did not come right out and say yes, but he did make note of the fact that the injury obviously affected Lamonica, and that he would have welcomed the chance to try and pull out a victory. Blanda, a confident man, said that he felt had he played he could have won, which was really just faith in himself, but the press used his quotes, some of which were surreptitiously taped by a reporter hanging out with Blanda and his friends after the game. Al Davis called him on the carpet. He broached no trouble within his ranks, but the owner recognized that it was Blanda's competitive nature, not criticism. Blanda and Lamonica competed for the coveted QB job, but they respected each other immensely, and helped each other.

Despite Lamonica's injury, the truth is that, had he been healthy, it may not have mattered. In the second regular season game between the two teams, Oakland won 10–6 to sweep the season series from K.C. But the score indicated that the two teams were so familiar with each other that the games resembled a stalemate, like the Brits and Germans locked in trench struggle during the Great War.

In 1970, Oakland found themselves in the new American Football Conference. The new alignment took some getting used to. Both the AFC and NFC were part of an overall National Football League, and they played an inter-conference schedule.

Oakland got off to a bad start when Paul Brown's Cincinnati Bengals, just a few years removed from expansion, upset them in the opener. Lamonica was inconsistent. It seemed that defensive coordinators had caught up to "the Mad Bomber."

Blanda missed a chip field goal against San Diego in a tie game. After three contests, the Raiders were a disastrous 0–2–1. Davis openly second-guessed coach John Madden. But Oakland came back to go unbeaten over the next seven games. In one of those games, Blanda replaced an injured Lamonica and threw three touchdowns in a 31–14 win but, as Ronald Reagan famously said, "You ain't seen nothin' yet."

For the Raiders, playing at Kansas City's Memorial Stadium was like entering the Roman Colosseum to do battle with uncaged lions. The 1970 grudge match was just such a gladiatorial death struggle!

The two teams got into a furious brawl, described in vivid detail by Bill King. King tried to describe who was hitting whom. Mainly Chiefs wide receiver Otis Taylor and Raider behemoth Ben Davidson had dagger eyes for each other (a matchup Taylor had no business engaging in). But as the free-for-all grew, King just threw up his hands and told his listeners he could no longer identify all the culprits.

With the score 17–14 Kansas City, the fight worked to Oakland's advantage. Davidson had hit Chief quarterback Len Dawson late and out of bounds. Davidson was flagged with an unsportsmanlike penalty, and Taylor was tossed out of the game. Madden and Dan Conners argued that Taylor's ejection was not enough, that Kansas City should be penalized on the ground, too. The argument worked, causing Kansas City to retry a third-down play after negating Dawson's first-down run. They failed the second time. The Raiders got the ball back with just enough time for Blanda to try a desperation 48-yarder, which was true, salvaging a 17–17 tie.

HALL OF FAMERS

Nineteen Raiders have been elected to the Pro Football Hall of Fame in Canton, Ohio. They are (including assistant coaches):

Name (years)	Position	Year elected
Jim Otto (1960–1974)	Center	1980
George Blanda (1967–1975)	Quarterback/kicker	1981
Willie Brown (1967–1978)	Cornerback	1984
Gene Upshaw (1967–1981)	Guard	1987
Fred Biletnikoff (1965–1978)	Wide receiver	1988
Art Shell (1968–1982)	Tackle	1989
Ted Hendricks (1975–1983)	Linebacker	1990
Al Davis (1963–present)	Owner/coach	1992
Bill Walsh (1966)	Assistant coach	1993
Joe Gibbs (1969–1970)	Assistant coach	1996
Mike Haynes (1983–1989)	Cornerback	1997
Eric Dickerson (1992)	Running back	1999
Howie Long (1981–1993)	Defensive end	2000
Ronnie Lott (1991–1992)	Safety	2000
Dave Casper (1974–1980, 1984)	Tight end	2002
Marcus Allen (1982–1992)	Running back	2003
James Lofton (1987–1988)	Wide receiver	2003
Bob Brown (1971–1973)	Offensive tackle	2004
John Madden (1969–1978)	Head coach	2006

Then Cleveland came to the Coliseum. Lamonica was ineffective, so Blanda was brought in to play quarterback. Trailing 20–13 late in the fourth quarter, Blanda passed to Warren Wells for a game-tying touchdown. It looked to be another tie, but a desperate interception gave Oakland the ball again. Blanda hit Hewritt Dixon for a short gain, giving him a shot at a 52-yard field goal with seven seconds left.

King judged his chances at "76 million to one-half," but when Blanda came through, he indeed was "*king of the world!*" Blanda's "relief pitcher" heroics proved decisive in Oakland's late, close wins over Denver (24–19) and San Diego (20–17). At Shea Stadium on a cold December day, it was Lamonica's Hail Mary to Wells that tied the game, 13–13, but George's extra point won it, 14–13.

Oakland was 8–4–2, good for the Western Division title in 1970. They lost to Baltimore in the conference championship game. It was not one of their great seasons, yet it remains one of their most truly memorable. It was the autumn of George Blanda, who made every man over the age of 40 proud. People who had no interest in the Raiders when they were 13–1 found a vulnerable 8–4–2 club irresistible.

Blanda stuck around into his mid-forties, finally retiring after the 1975 season. His relief appearances were never as frequent after 1970. Eventually Ken Stabler took over the position, removing any question over who the quarterback should be. Sadly, Blanda was not a member of the 1976 Super Bowl championship team, but he goes down in history as one of the all-time great Raiders.

"THE SEA OF HANDS"

When Raider fans discuss their all-time great teams, there are many to choose from. Certainly the 1967–1969 squads were juggernauts. The 1976 champions and two Super Bowl winners of the 1980s come to mind. But the 1974 Raiders were as good as any of them, which demonstrates why their failure to bring home the brass ring was such a source of frustration.

Ken Stabler entered the campaign in his prime. He had performed magnificently—albeit with some inconsistency—in 1973 and had the job all the way, having completed a stupendous 62.7 percent of his passes in his first full year.

Coach Madden and the fans also had confidence that he was a gutsy performer who could be counted on in the fourth quarter of close games. First-round draft pick Henry Lawrence came to Oakland after having played at tiny Florida A&M. Davis and his scouts were unafraid of choosing lesser-known players from traditionally black colleges, and they usually chose right. In Lawrence's case, most definitely.

Speedy wide receiver Cliff Branch was always a threat to go long. He averaged better than 17 yards per catch during a 14-year career with the Raiders, during which he amassed 501 receptions—67 for touchdowns.

But the key pick came in the form of the number-two choice. This one was hardly hidden in a low-profile program. Tight end Dave Casper helped lead Notre Dame to the 1973 national title. Casper's role would represent a paradigm shift in Raider—and pro football—mentality. The old AFL "Mad Bomber" days were long gone. While nobody was yet calling it the "West Coast offense," that is what it was.

Tight ends had traditionally been blockers, but in recent years more athletic performers were playing the position. John Mackey had revolutionized the position with Johnny Unitas and Earl Morrall at Baltimore. USC's Charle Young had seemingly directed the spotlight at his position through sheer force of will and extraordinary talent.

Casper could block, he could catch, and he could run after the catch. No longer was the option confined to the long pass or the run. The "tight end option," or indeed planned pass plays to tight ends and running backs, was now fully implemented into NFL playbooks. Casper made up for Ray Chester's departure.

Mark van Eeghen became Oakland's *second running back from Colgate,* which was an unlikely scenario. If Davis and his scouts were to be believed, the little liberal arts college was the "Fullback U" of the East Coast. Davis supposedly "discovered" van Eeghen working out in a gym and noticed his leg strength.

Hopes were high, but O.J. Simpson and Buffalo upended Oakland in the *Monday Night Football* opener at Rich Stadium.

OVERTIME

Hall of Fame tight end Dave Casper's nickname was "Ghost" because he could "disappear," and also because of the comic character, Casper the Friendly Ghost. In the 1977 AFC playoff game between the Raiders and Baltimore Colts, it was Casper's 10-yard touchdown reception that ended the double-overtime affair, 37–31, in favor of the Raiders. "Ghost to the Post" refers to Casper's 42-yard reception route, setting up the tying field goal at the end of regulation.

Stabler and Madden sensed that the Bills could not keep up with their club, but possessed in Simpson enough firepower to scare them into changing the game plan. Oakland maintained a conservative approach, which seemed to be working in the fourth quarter, but in retrospect had they let the "dogs out" they may have been winning by enough to offset the late-game heroics of Joe Ferguson and Ahmad Rashad in the Bills' surprise 21–20 win.

After that, however, with all the pistons greased, Oakland stepped up with nine straight victories. With each successive win, the Stabler-to-Casper connection became more important. Kansas City, an also-ran by now, fell 27–7. Oakland's 17–0 shutout of Pittsburgh at Three Rivers Stadium was felt by many to identify a huge shift in pro football fortunes.

Terry Bradshaw had shown brilliance and inconsistency throughout his career. Joe Gilliam replaced him. Oakland's stifling defeat of the Steelers in their home stadium signaled that Davis's team had arrived, and the Steelers seemingly had passed their chance.

Clarence Davis dominated with 116 yards rushing in a 40–24 pasting of the Browns. Both Cliff Branch and Bob Moore caught TD passes in a 14–10 win over San Diego. Davis again led the team in a stirring 30–27 victory over Cincinnati.

Oakland crossed the bridge, knocking the 49ers off at Candlestick Park. In so doing, they assumed the alpha male position of Bay Area grid supremacy (in confluence with the baseball A's, who won their third straight World Series that fall while the Giants bumbled along). San Francisco fell 35–24. Stabler's 64-yarder to Branch keyed the win.

Denver lost 28–17 when Stabler connected for four TD passes, including a 61-yard longball to Branch, who added two more the following week in a 35–13 destruction of Detroit.

Branch added to his bid for superstardom with no less than seven catches, one for a score, in a victory over San Diego that clinched the division championship. With the title under wraps, Madden rested his starters in a 20–17 loss to the Broncos, but the Raiders notched it back up down the stretch, not wanting to get stale for the playoffs.

Stabler threw four TD passes in a 41–26 victory over Jim Plunkett and New England, with Skip Thomas picking one errant Plunkett toss and taking it all the way back for a score. Otis Sistrunk keyed a 7–6 win over Kansas City, sacking Lenny Dawson and recovering his fumble. Old man Blanda played QB, tossing a touchdown pass in addition to kicking two field goals and three conversions in the first-ever meeting between legendary franchises—Oakland coming out on top of Dallas, 27–23.

The game was played on a Saturday night, but covered by the regular *Monday Night Football* crew of Howard Cosell, "Dandy Don" Meredith, and Frank Gifford. Oakland had a big lead but relaxed while the desperate Cowboys, who needed a win in order to make the playoffs, fought to avoid their first early exit since 1965. When Dallas made it close toward the end, the camera focused on Raider players and coaches enjoying themselves on the bench, leading Cosell to remark on their "cavalier" attitude. But in the end, they prevailed.

"[THE RAIDERS HAVE] BEATEN THE BEST TEAM IN PRO FOOTBALL TODAY."

—JOHN MADDEN, AFTER THE "SEA OF HANDS" PLAYOFF VICTORY OVER THE DOLPHINS

The playoffs offered the prospect of old dragons lined up for slaying—with it, all the old doubts and insecurities in one big bowl of revenge and dominance asserted. It would not be easy, for sure.

Enter Miami, 11–3, fully loaded with the cast of stars who had propelled Don Shula's team to the previous three Super Bowls. The media made it clear that this was the "real" Super Bowl. The game matched expectations.

Nat Moore returned the opening kick 89 yards for a touchdown, shutting the Raider faithful right up. Stabler was up to the reply, driving Oakland 89 yards, capped by a 31-yard TD pass to Charlie Smith, tying it at 7–7. The two teams fought each other like Joe Frazier and Muhammad Ali, the lead seesawing back and forth until the fourth quarter, when the Dolphins forged ahead, 26–21.

It was vintage Stabler, methodically driving his desperate team upfield. Announcer Bill King was going crazy, describing how close the Raiders were to the veritable "Promised Land," just yards away. But the two teams had fought for every inch of real estate all afternoon. Miami defended these last inches with the same tenacity as Joshua Chamberlain's 20th Maine holding Little Round Top at Gettysburg.

This time, God—or somebody—was with the rebels.

With 35 seconds remaining, Oakland had no timeouts. Stabler dropped back and was rushed fiercely, with Vern Den Herder hitting him hard. Falling, his knee *inches* from the ground, Snake got a desperate pass off. His target: Clarence Davis, surrounded by a "sea of hands" in the form of Dolphin defenders. They needed to knock the ball away without committing pass interference. Linebacker Mike Kolen had hold of Davis's jersey, but somehow amid all those hands and aqua defenders, Davis held the ball for the miracle 28–26 victory, thus ensuring his place in the happy hearts of the Raider Nation for time immemorial.

The Raiders then made one of their biggest mistakes. They lost their "pride and poise." With the Coliseum in full bedlam, the team joyously made their way into the locker room amid a celebration that had all the earmarks of a Super Bowl victory party, with little immediate consideration for the fact that they had to win another playoff game just to advance to the final game.

The media pressed them with questions that had the ring of, "What's it like to finally win the big one?" before they had gone all the way. Gene Upshaw was just happy that "something like that went our way in the playoffs. Usually that's the kind of thing that goes against us."

"I hope Oakland goes all the way," remarked Miami coach Don Shula.

But it was John Madden, normally smarter than this, who made the mistake of telling the press the Raiders had "beaten the best team in pro football today," which meant that his team was now the best in pro football.

In Pittsburgh, Pennsylvania, the Steelers heard and absorbed every word. The odds were against them. They had been shut out by Oakland at Three Rivers Stadium earlier in the season, and had lost to them soundly in the 1973 playoffs. The revenge factor had still not worn off after "the Immaculate Reception," and the game

RIVALRIES

The Raiders faltered to archrival Pittsburgh in the AFC Championship Game in 1974, perhaps their most galling defeat. Had they won, they most surely would have beaten Minnesota in the Super Bowl, giving the city of Oakland that rarest of pro trifectas: three World Championships in a one-year period. The A's won the World Series in October and in the spring of '75 the Warriors won the NBA title. Between January 1969 and May 1970, the New York Jets, Mets, and Knicks won three titles. In 1972 the Los Angeles Lakers, UCLA basketball, and USC football won titles.

was at the Coliseum. No ice, no snowstorms, no freezing artificial carpet, just California sunshine for a California team on California grass.

It was not even close. The Steelers outclassed Oakland, their pass rush blitzing Stabler all day long, while Franco Harris and Rocky Bleier cranked out big gains. The Raiders led 10–3, but in the fourth quarter Pittsburgh separated the men from the boys with three scores to win 24–13.

"Just use the same quotes from last year," said Marv Hubbard. "Every damn year it's like this. We had everything in our favor. We had them in our stadium, in front of our fans, on grass, coming off that great game last week. It just wasn't in the cards this year, again. When will it be?"

"Defeat is a bitch," Madden said.

Over the previous decades, the Brooklyn Dodgers' "next year" came in 1955. The Dallas Cowboys silenced the critics with their 1972 Super Bowl victory, and that same year the previously snakebit Lakers finally won an NBA title. The Raiders had exclusive membership in a dubious club, it seemed. The glare of the national spotlight was on them, and it was not kind.

"HOME OF CHAMPIONS"

The 1967 Raiders were not quite ready, their flaws exposed by Green Bay. The 1968 and 1969 teams may have been the best in football, but upsets at the hands of the New York Jets and Kansas City Chiefs denied them their "rightful" place. The 1970 and 1971 teams were competent but down by Raider standards, and in 1972 Oakland was Super Bowl–worthy, but nobody would rate them higher than that year's unbeaten Dolphins.

By 1973–1974, however, the frustration level for Davis, Madden, and the fans was at an all-time high. Oakland was as good as anybody in pro football, but they failed when the pressure was on, in the AFC title game.

"JUST USE THE SAME QUOTES FROM LAST YEAR. EVERY DAMN YEAR IT'S LIKE THIS. WE HAD EVERYTHING IN OUR FAVOR. WE HAD THEM IN OUR STADIUM, IN FRONT OF OUR FANS, ON GRASS, COMING OFF THAT GREAT GAME LAST WEEK. IT JUST WASN'T IN THE CARDS THIS YEAR, AGAIN. WHEN WILL IT BE?"

—MARV HUBBARD, AFTER THE LOSS TO THE STEELERS THAT ENDED THE RAIDERS' GREAT 1974 SEASON

The 1973 Raiders were a solid club that suffered their share of ups and downs. In the end, the Dolphin team that knocked them out in the playoffs successfully defended their world championship. In 1974, Oakland had all cylinders clickin', only to lose to Pittsburgh in a disappointing championship match. In 1975, they fell in freezing weather at Three Rivers Stadium.

Davis had to sit idly by while the pro football gods anointed the title of all-time greatness on a new rival, the Steelers. Kansas City, the Jets, Miami, now Pittsburgh—when would it be their turn? When would Ken Stabler lead them to the Promised Land?

The Raiders' "wilderness years" ended in 1976. Everything fell into place. The stars were aligned just right. Ted Hendricks had been acquired from Green Bay. Charles Philyaw was drafted. Clarence Davis was still in his prime at running back. George Blanda finally retired at age 49. Jim Otto called it quits.

John "the Tooz" Matuszak came over to Oakland. The first pick in the 1973 Draft by Houston out of the University of Tampa, he had not settled in yet but found a home in wild and woolly Oakland.

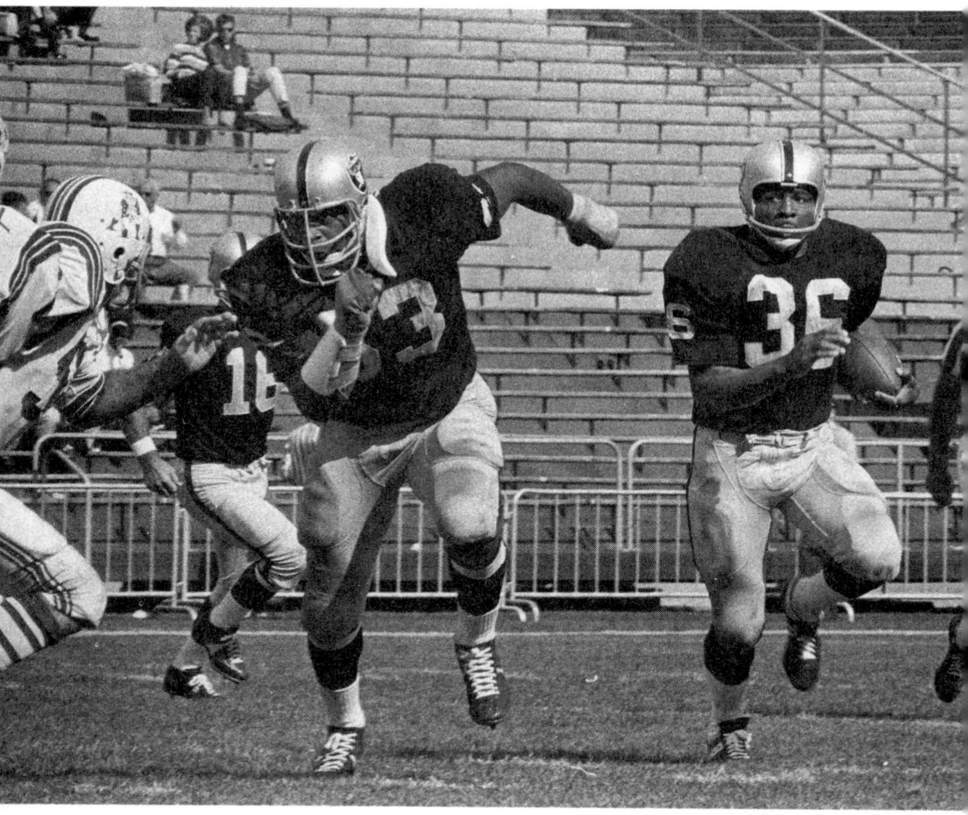

Halfback Clem Daniels (shown following the blocking of Gene Upshaw) was the Raiders' first star running back. He led the AFL in rushing in 1963 with 1,009 yards, earning him the first of four consecutive Pro Bowl berths.

Stabler and Biletnikoff were in their prime. Normally lackluster in the preseason, in 1976 Oakland was too strong to be beaten, whether it was an exhibition game or not. They opened at the Oakland Coliseum against the hated Steelers, and at first it looked ugly. But Stabler put on a patented fourth-quarter effort, directing the Raiders on two impressive drives draped around a blocked Steeler punt.

Heated feelings fomented on the field, with accusations about "criminality" flung around. In the end, Snake delivered an improbable 31–28 victory that set the tone for the entire season. From 1970 to 1975, Oakland had lost its season opener every year, an unlikely scenario considering they were constant contenders. But the first-game defeats proved to be a psychological barrier. A sense of inevitability had settled in: lose the opener, lose the last (playoff) game. Not in '76. With the two-time defending Super Bowl champions dispatched, Oakland got off to a 3–0 start. Still feeling their way, the Raiders were tested, 24–21 by Kansas City and 14–13 at Houston, when USC's Mike Rae had to sub for the injured Snake. Rae tossed two touchdown passes, including the game-winner to Cliff Branch.

Week four was terribly disappointing; a resounding 48–17 loss at New England. But after that, the team settled in and won 10 straight to close out the regular campaign 13–1. Stabler hit 67 percent of his passes to Branch, Biletnikoff, and Dave Casper. Davis and Mark van Eeghen gave the team just enough of a running attack to balance things out and allow them to play ball control when necessary. Pete Banaszak provided both blocking and short-yardage running.

The 1976 Raiders featured one of the greatest offensive lines in history. Old clips of Stabler show him sitting in the pocket virtually unharried while picking and choosing his targets. Against San Diego, Stabler threw three scoring strikes in the 27–17 win. Denver fell both times. In a 19–6 home victory, the Oakland defense stifled Bronco quarterback Steve Ramsey, sacking him 10 times to the delight of a packed Coliseum. Green Bay fought hard but was not able to match the Raiders on either side of the ball.

On November 7, the Raiders traveled to Soldier Field. The Bears were average in 1976, but the crowd was out for blood on a chilly Windy City day. They almost got it,

TOP 10

Greatest Pro Football Teams of the Super Bowl Era (1966–Present)

1. 1972 Miami Dolphins
2. 1985 Chicago Bears
3. 1984 San Francisco 49ers
4. **1976 Oakland Raiders**
5. 1966 Green Bay Packers
6. 1978 Pittsburgh Steelers
7. 1989 San Francisco 49ers
8. 1986 New York Giants
9. 1977 Dallas Cowboys
10. 1999 St. Louis Rams

but in the end the magic of 1976 could not be denied. Stabler and Company prevailed by the thinnest of margins, 28–27. Branch was the hero, streaking through the Chicago secondary to catch two big passes.

In a 21–10 win over Kansas City, Casper and Biletnikoff were the dominant stars. Philadelphia was outgunned, 26–7. Eagle quarterback Roman Gabriel, a one-time NFL Most Valuable Player with the Rams, looked over the hill as he was flattened repeatedly. Van Eeghen spurred a ball-control offense in the division-clinching win.

Poor John McKay, who had dominated college football at Southern California for years, was in over his head as coach of the expansion Tampa Bay Buccaneers, who fell 49–16. Stabler connected on a touchdown pass, as did the man who led McKay's Trojans to the 1972 national championship, Raider backup Mike Rae. Asked what he "thought of his team's execution," McKay said wryly that he thought it was "a good idea."

Week 13 featured Oakland versus the tough Cincinnati Bengals on *Monday Night Football*. The Bengals were battling Pittsburgh for the AFC Central Division crown, and a Cincinnati victory could possibly knock the Steelers out of the postseason. Grumbling from Pittsburgh held that Oakland would give up in a meaningless game to them in order to assure they not have to face the Steel Curtain later.

Instead, Stabler hit on all cylinders, mostly to Branch and Biletnikoff. Oakland cruised to a 35–20 win. Casper made it to the end zone twice, while Bengal quarterback Ken Anderson was intercepted three times.

GOING CAMPING

When "Large Charles" Philyaw first saw Mark van Eeghen in training camp, he asked why he was the only player to have his first name on the back of his jersey. He thought his first name was "Van," not Mark. Philyaw was replaced by 6'8", 280-pound John Matuszak at left end in 1976.

Stabler rested on the last week of the regular season, but Rae continued to look capable of leading them if necessary in a resounding 24–0 whitewashing of the Chargers. Van Eeghen passed the 1,000-yard rushing mark with a 95-yard performance against San Diego. When it was all said and done, Pittsburgh came all the way back from a bad start to win the Central. Oakland's defeat of Cincinnati ultimately had the effect of knocking the Bengals out and propelling their archrivals into a likely confrontation with the Silver and Black, for the ultimate prize.

The 1976 regular season completed an amazing 10-year run in which Oakland won 108 games against only 25 defeats and seven ties, an .796 winning percentage that represented the best decade in pro football history. They had accomplished all there was to accomplish, with one exception.

SNAKE

In the 1960s, Alabama football coach Paul "Bear" Bryant made a speech to a group of California high school football coaches.

"Send your A students to Cal and Stanford," he told them. "They'll get a fine education. Send your B students to USC or UCLA. Hell, I'd send my own kin there. Send you're C students to one of your fine state universities. But send yer whiskey-drinkin', skirt-chasin' D students to ol' Bear, and I'll turn 'em into football players."

The coaches looked at each other and laughed, because they knew that Bear had already taken a couple of those "whiskey-drinkin', skirt-chasin' D students," turning Joe Willie Namath and Kenny Stabler into great football players.

The Alabama that Stabler played at was segregated, mired in the controversy of the 1960s. But times, they were a-changin'. Namath came to 'Bama from Beaver Falls, Pennsylvania. Sylvester Croom, who later played for Bryant and became the first black coach in the SEC at Mississippi State, was a teenager when Namath arrived at Alabama.

"Namath would show up unannounced, by himself, in the black neighborhoods of Tuscaloosa," recalled Croom in *One Night,*

Two Teams: Alabama vs. USC and the Game That Changed a Nation. "He would glad-hand black folks. It was surreal. He was like a cool jazz singer."

Indeed, Namath was the "New Breed" of 1960s athlete in America. His successor, Stabler, was cut out of the same cloth. Kenny came from humble rural beginnings on the Alabama Gulf Coast, which Snake dubbed the "Redneck Riviera." His father liked to take the family to a local honky-tonk on Saturday nights, where he would drink and play guitar.

DID YOU KNOW...

That Dave Casper would visit Ken Stabler in Lower Alabama for summertime "fishing trips"? One hot day, they departed a roadhouse on Highway 182 but mishandled a Styrofoam cooler containing a pound of live shrimp, which fell on the sizzling asphalt and started to cook! Stabler said the flock of seagulls and blackbirds that descended on the shrimp—and them—was "like a scene from an Alfred Hitchcock movie."

Stabler was recruited to play at 'Bama, but quickly ran afoul of Bryant. He was not a good student, partied heavily, and ran a swath through the campus female population, eventually earning a suspension from Bear.

"I drove back to Tuscaloosa drinking beer and throwing the empties out the side of the window," Stabler said of his return to school after serving the suspension. "The more I drank and thought, the more I decided to toe the line."

Perhaps this was not perfect penitence, but it was enough. Stabler and Bryant managed to come to a truce.

"Coach Bryant respected Kenny," said former Alabama assistant coach Clem Gryska in *One Night, Two Teams*, "because he was always ready to play on game day, and never backed down from a challenge. He was his kind of player."

In 1966, Snake led the Crimson Tide to an undefeated, untied season and a Sugar Bowl victory. In the controversial "Catholic vote," the national championship was awarded not to Alabama, but to Notre Dame, despite their having tied Michigan State. *L.A. Times* columnist Jim Murray led the "boycott" of all-white Alabama because they did not play integrated teams north of the

Ken "Snake" Stabler was known as much for his hard-partying lifestyle as for his skills as a quarterback—but those were considerable. The left-handed passer won 100 games during his first 150 contests as the Raiders' starter.

Mason-Dixon Line and did not deserve national accolades so long as they were segregated.

"The players, however, were ready for integration," said Scott Hunter, who succeeded Stabler as Alabama's quarterback. Clarence Davis, who was born in Birmingham but not able to play for the Tide, later said that he never had problems with Snake.

Stabler had an easygoing mentality. When he got to the pro game, which of course was totally integrated—especially Al Davis's teams—there was never any hint of racial problems between him and his teammates. They all just headed to the local saloon and partied together as "equal opportunity enjoyers."

Today, the best bar scene in the Bay Area can be found in the Walnut Creek area. Many A's and Raiders players live in the comfortable neighborhoods of Walnut Creek, Danville, Pleasanton, and thereabouts. But in the 1970s, this area was much less developed than it is today.

Stabler and his pals made use of the seedier joints that occupied the old Oakland downtown and waterfront—the Airport Hyatt Hotel lounge, blue-collar dives in Hayward and San Leandro. In Santa Rosa, they cooled off from the 100-degree training camp heat with frosty cold ones in the country and biker establishments that make up that unique corner of America. Everywhere they went, attractive, semi-attractive, and unattractive women found them.

Women who followed the Raiders tended to be a different breed from most pro sports groupies. In New York and L.A., Joe Namath and Fred Dryer were hanging out with high-class models and Playmates at Hugh Hefner's mansion. The Raider girls tended to be more *Easy Rider* than *Playboy*. It was the middle of the sexual revolution, years before anybody ever heard of AIDS. Kenny and his pals just took one big scoop of life's bowl of ice cream—in all flavors.

Raiderette cheerleaders tended to either have a stripper allure to them or looked like Shattuck Avenue streetwalkers—wild, thigh-high boots, hot pants, and attitude. The NFL imposed no restrictions on player-cheerleader fraternization, as they do today. One blonde Raiderette posed in the nude, bragging about her experiences with Stabler and other players, engendering orgiastic fantasies in the minds of readers. Then Stabler did an outrageous, soft-porn sexspread for a gentlemen's magazine with famed San Francisco stripper Carol Doda. Had he been on any other team (Lombardi's Packers, Landry's Cowboys), he might have been shipped off the farm. With the Raiders, it just made for a few laughs. Madden did not care. Davis did not care. If he threw for touchdowns on Sunday, they did not care how much he scored on Saturday.

Stabler's off-field exploits in Oakland and on the road were nothing compared to his lifestyle in Lower Alabama, which is a coastal region sitting on the Gulf of Mexico. It is a stretch of waterfront bars, honky tonks, strip clubs, tattoo parlors, fishing trawlers, off-shore gambling casinos, house boats, and all other shady endeavors. It is Kenny Stabler's world, and he is welcome to it.

In high school, Stabler was also a baseball star who squared off against another diamond stud of the region, Don Sutton (later of the Dodgers). Stabler returned to L.A. (Lower Alabama) every spring. The steaming hot summers were not devoted to weight training, long passing and wind-sprint sessions at the local high school, or much of anything else. By and large Kenny spent 90 percent of his time on wine, women, and song, wasting the other 10 percent of it.

With drunk driving apparently more a sport than a crime in those days, Snake and his nefarious pals hit haunt after haunt, shooting pool, drinkin' beer, downing shots, and wooing the half-dressed cowgirls of the Alabama summer. This is a state that sits in the Bible Belt. Apparently the denizens of Lower 'Bama were making an in-depth study of sin.

Stabler was married several times, "but my wives never took kindly to my not comin' home for several days at a time." His most memorable squeeze was a local gal, reportedly a stripper—or something like a stripper—known by the moniker "Wickedly Wonderful" Wanda. Stabler said that when he failed to appear for days at a time, she was likely to greet his homecoming with buckshot or some other violent means.

Many are amazed to discover that Snake is *not* in the Hall of Fame. He will be.

THINGS TO SAVOR

After the Raiders won the Super Bowl, a sign started to appear in Oakland at the Oakland Airport and at the Oakland–Alameda County Coliseum. It read "Oakland: Home of Champions." In the 1970s, the city was host to three baseball World Champions (A's, 1972–1974), one in football (Raiders, 1976) and one in basketball (Warriors, 1975).

THE BEST SLOW HALL OF FAME RECEIVER MONEY CAN BUY

Football is a game of big, fast super-athletes. Every once in a while, a comparatively slow wide receiver comes along. But the receiver position is one in which a shifty, smart guy with moves can succeed even if he is not particularly fast or big. Raymond Berry of the Baltimore Colts fit this profile perfectly. Fred Biletnikoff followed in that tradition.

"Fred Biletnikoff plays football the way the Cossacks used to fight wars," wrote sportswriter Wells Twombly.

It was a hard slog at first. Biletnikoff came out of Florida State in the second round of the 1965 Draft, at a time when the Raiders were not yet a dynasty, although they had established themselves as a passing offense to be reckoned with.

In his first year, Fred dropped pass after pass. It got so bad that he contacted the New York Yankees, who had previously offered him a contract to play baseball, but in the end he decided to "stick" with football.

Biletnikoff was a hardnose, one of Stabler's drinking buddies off the field and a man inextricably linked to Snake by their on-field offensive heroics. Biletnikoff was not intimidated by anybody.

Biletnikoff has been called a "self-taught pass catcher" who surpassed speedsters of his era, like Dallas's Bob Hayes and Miami's Paul Warfield. Lance Alworth of the San Diego Chargers and Gene Washington of the San Francisco 49ers had great leaping ability, which Biletnikoff lacked, but the Raider

TOP 10

Greatest Quarterback-Receiver Combinations

1. Joe Montana to Jerry Rice
2. Terry Bradshaw to Lynn Swann
3. Johnny Unitas to Raymond Berry
4. Troy Aikman to Michael Irvin
5. **Kenny Stabler to Fred Biletnikoff**
6. Sammy Baugh to Don Hutson
7. Joe Namath to Don Maynard
8. Len Dawson to Otis Taylor
9. Dan Fouts to John Jefferson
10. Bob Griese to Paul Warfield

RIVALRIES

In the 1960s, the Raiders and Jets had it in for each other. Joe Namath and New York beat Oakland 27–23 in the 1968 AFL championship game. Daryle Lamonica threw for 401 yards,190 of those to Fred Biletnikoff.

receiver was better than those two stalwarts. Don Maynard of the New York Jets and Otis Taylor of the Kansas City Chiefs had better hands, at least until Biletnikoff discovered stickum.

In the beginning, Biletnikoff got off to a bad start, suffering knee surgery that cost him the starting job to the heralded USC star, Rod Sherman.

"That's when I decided to go to work," said Biletnikoff. "If I didn't have great speed, I'd just have to figure out some other way to run deep. I've always been quick. My moves are faster than my feet. So I have to take advantage of what God gave me."

Biletnikoff was a quirky personality who would chew his fingernails. Prior to games, he would always go to the training room and throw up. Before Stabler came along, Biletnikoff and Daryle Lamonica made up one of the best, if not *the* best, quarterback-receiver combinations in the game.

"Frankly, I don't think he's that slow," said Lamonica. "I've been hearing that ever since I started throwing to Fred. I saw him tie Warren Wells in a 40-yard dash once, and Warren could fly. He always knows where the ball is and he can get to it. Maybe Fred's fast and the ground just moves underneath him."

Biletnikoff, despite his devil-may-care attitude, was always a hard worker who spent many extra hours on the practice field, then worked out with a punching bag in the offseasons. His hand-eye coordination was second to none, which he credited to the punching-bag routine.

One of his great traits was to slow up under a pass, thus juking the defender away from him, giving him open space to make the catch. Biletnikoff became the all-time leading receiver in Raider history with 598 career receptions, fourth among all pro receivers

Fred Biletnikoff (shown with buddy Ken Stabler) lacked speed, was a heavy smoker, and loaded his hands with stickum, but he was one of football's all-time-great possession receivers. His remarkable 14-year career with the Raiders earned him a spot in the NFL Hall of Fame.

at the time of his retirement. He caught 76 career touchdowns in addition to 70 passes for 1,167 yards in postseason games (second in NFL history). Biletnikoff was the Most Valuable Player of Super Bowl XI in 1977, when he nabbed four Stabler passes for 79 yards. He caught 40 or more passes for a record 10 straight years (1967–1976).

Biletnikoff in many ways symbolized the Raiders. He never played on a losing team after having set records at Florida State, helping to build the Seminoles into the collegiate power they eventually became. Biletnikoff was named to the Walter Camp All-Century Team, and returned to the Raiders in 1989, holding several positions over the years. The annual award that goes to the best college wide receiver in the nation is named after Biletnikoff. He was named to the Pro Football Hall of Fame in 1988.

Biletnikoff, along with several other Raiders, was notorious for using stickum on his hands to help catch the football. The substance would get all over the ball, plus everything he picked up stuck to his hands, sometimes even after the game. He was, of course, a favorite of Davis. Being from Florida, which is next to Alabama, Biletnikoff and Stabler seemed to bond—easy-going, cantankerous at times, fun loving, and absolutely competitive.

In the pantheon of all-time great receivers, Biletnikoff would get plenty of supporters arguing that he is the best of them all. Generally, San Francisco 49er superstar Jerry Rice is thought to be the best. Tim Brown, who came to the Raiders a decade after Biletnikoff, is worthy of mention. Biletnikoff undoubtedly is on the shortest, most elite of the lists.

IT AIN'T OVER 'TIL IT'S OVER

COMMITMENT TO EXCELLENCE

In the year 2008, many myths and urban legends have been spread about the aging Al Davis and his Raider empire. Many of these stories are told by younger fans whose memories of the team extend no further than the Jim Plunkett Super Bowl team of 1980, or maybe even the later Los Angeles years.

The truth is, the "commitment to excellence," the "pride and poise," and the "greatness that is the Raiders," as Davis likes to call it, stem as much from a period (1967–1969) in which the team did *not* win one of their three Super Bowls, yet remains a golden age in Raider lore.

The 1967 Raiders, indeed, put Oakland on the map. Among history's great pro teams, the '67 team is not mentioned, although they could have beaten many subsequent Super Bowl winners. The same can be said of the 1968–1969 Raiders, yet they suffer the same, increasingly frustrating malady which, at the time, varied between "choking" and an inability to "win the big one."

This is not an uncommon malfunction in the sports world. The Brooklyn Dodgers always had to "wait 'til next year," until 1955. Then, in the 1960s they took up a comfortable residence in the Promised Land: California 90012.

Consequently, their rival, the New York Giants, who had captured the brass ring five times in the Big Apple, found themselves playing defeated Philistines to L.A.'s Chosen People for

> **TRIVIA**
>
> What was the Raiders' scoring total over opponents in 1967?
>
> Find the answers on page 177.

more than 50 years in the Golden State.

The Los Angeles Rams came into existence and found winning to be just as easy as existing. They moved west from Cleveland in 1946, and in 1951 they won the title, but then endured almost 50 "wilderness years" and half a continent's journey until they stumbled upon Super Bowl success in St. Louis.

The team that replaced the Rams as the "next big thing," the Cleveland Browns, won numerous titles with Paul and Jim Brown before putting their fans through agonizing years of near-misses until, indignity of indignities, they won for the greater glory of...Baltimore.

The Los Angeles Lakers seemingly played the Washington Generals to the Boston Celtics' Harlem Globetrotters in the 1960s, until 1972. The Dallas Cowboys were the NFL version of the AFL Raiders: fireworks, fury, and playoff losses, until the 1971 season. The Raiders' archenemies, the Denver Broncos, lost four Super Bowls before John Elway transformed himself from disappointment to football god. The Boston Red Sox (1918–2004) and Chicago White Sox (1917–2005) appeared to have been under some kind of 20th-century curse. Everybody, or so it sometimes seems, eventually wins. The Anaheim Angels' 2002 championship would appear to be evidence of that, but there are exceptions.

The San Diego Chargers have never won a Super Bowl. At least Buffalo went to four in a row from 1991 to 1994, albeit never returning to a victory parade, which leaves us with the kings of sports failure: the Chicago Cubs (last world championship, 1908). In retrospect, the Raiders' wilderness period, which actually did not end until they conquered the Rose Bowl in Pasadena in the manner of Patton taking Palermo in 1977, seems fairly short when compared to some of the longer sports droughts.

But the California fan is a hybrid. Fans in Boston and Chicago are the sports versions of Chinese political leaders, who think in terms of centuries, not years or decades. (Chinese premier Chou

En-lai, asked in 1972 about the effects of the 1789 French Revolution, said, "It's still too early to tell.") Raider defeats at the hands of the Packers, Jets, Chiefs, Colts, Steelers, and Dolphins between 1968 and 1976 added up to what seemed at the time an eternity.

It was not just losing. It was the way they lost on the heels of so much success, for among those fall-short teams are some of the greatest also-rans in the history of the game. The 1968–1969 Raiders, in particular, represent so much sheer talent and potential that their season-ending defeats are still galling in memory. From 1967 to 1969, Oakland was 37–4–1 in regular-season play. They won playoff games the way the Wehrmacht took France in 1940, but then played Napoleon at Waterloo, Hitler at Stalingrad, and Hannibal outside Rome, each in successive years.

Under John Rauch, the Raiders were 12–2 in 1968. This was the pinnacle year for the American Football League. Baltimore won the NFL title with a 13–1 record, but they probably were no better than the fourth-best team in the AFL. Coach Hank Stram's Kansas City Chiefs, led by quarterback Len Dawson, were also 12–2. Then there were the New York Jets, seemingly a "close but no cigar" 11–3.

The Raiders *owned* the Bay Area. Every game was sold out, and getting tickets was harder than Chinese math. Home games could not be televised, not even playoffs. The awesome descriptions of the great Bill King emanated from seemingly every radio in every home, office, and car. To those who came of age anywhere in the old 415 or the 408, this was the most lasting memory.

The 49ers were a joke, their stadium a wreck. More people showed up to hear free concerts (complete with

DID YOU KNOW...

That assistant coach Bill Walsh took over the semipro San Jose Apaches in 1967? That left a staff opening. John Madden, the linebackers coach under Don Coryell at San Diego State, was brought in. If Walsh hadn't left, the team's future and character might have taken on a different complexion.

acid-induced "Summer of Love" nudity) in Golden Gate Park than ventured into rickety Kezar. The *Oakland Tribune*, of course, continued to be the Raider mouthpiece, but the *San Francisco Chronicle*, the *Examiner*, and the *San Jose Mercury News* jumped on their bandwagon feet first, led by the likes of Glenn Dickey, Art Spander, and Wells Twombly.

They were a force to be reckoned with, the ultimate Al Davis concoction of fear, intimidation, and trickery. Davis continued to play the draft, to quote King, "like Heifetz." Ken Stabler of Alabama improbably was still available in the second round. Another player from a black college, Art Shell of Maryland State, came on board. Charlie Smith from Utah was chosen. George Atkinson was discovered out of little Morris Brown College. Colgate's Marv Hubbard became a Raider. Players from black colleges, small schools, and renegades from Lynyrd Skynyrd concerts were not the only people Davis found. He loved USC, considering it a breeding ground for pro stardom ever since he coached there. Linebacker Chip Oliver, not a star with the Trojans, was picked in 1968 and became a key team player.

Oakland lost to San Diego and Kansas City in 1968, but avenged the Chiefs in an easy home win, won a memorable game against New York, and then destroyed Kansas City in a special playoff. Lamonica fired five touchdown passes, three to Florida State's Fred Biletnikoff, to fuel a 41–6 win. They looked to be the favorites to make a repeat Super Bowl trip, again to Miami.

There was no automatic home-field advantage to be gained by having the better regular-season record, so on a cold, blustery December day, Oakland had to venture into Shea Stadium.

Lamonica threw for 401 yards, but Atkinson met his match in the form of the Jets' deadly combination of Joe Namath–to–Don Maynard. Maynard caught two TD passes, but Lamonica drove Oakland to a score, making it 23–20 Raiders. Namath went to work, leading his team on a touchdown drive, but Daryle had time to work his magic. His place in Raider history was tarnished on a play that symbolized the long years of frustration when he lost his poise and made some kind of errant "throw" that fell somewhere between a fumble and a non-forward pass. Ralph

Running back Charlie Smith was an effective receiver out of the backfield for Oakland; he is shown hauling in a pass during a home game against the Browns. He played for the Raiders from 1968 to 1974, racking up nearly 5,000 yards of total offense.

Baker recovered the errant…lateral(?), and the Jets prevailed 27–23. When they beat Baltimore, they and "Broadway Joe" entered the pantheon of all-time New York greatness, which is as big as it gets.

Rauch could not figure out the funny little man from Brooklyn. Davis's control of head coaches was something never quite seen before. Rauch left and was replaced by an amiable

33-year-old from Daly City's Jefferson High School and the great collegiate football power that is Cal Poly San Luis Obispo: John Madden.

The beat, as Sonny and Cher were so musically informing the nation in 1969, went on: 12–1–1. Kansas City fell twice in the regular season. Defensive tackle Art Thoms of Syracuse and offensive guard George Buehler of Stanford joined the hit parade. Lamonica passed all season to Biletnikoff, Wells, and Charlie Smith. It was probably his best season. He earned MVP honors again, and in the playoffs hit Biletnikoff and Rod Sherman for two scores apiece in a devastating 56–7 rout of Houston.

But against the Chiefs in the AFL title game at the Coliseum, Lamonica injured his passing hand against the helmet of Kansas City's Aaron Brown. After striking first to lead 7–0, Oakland became impotent, unable to pick up on the defensive or offensive schemes of Hank Stram, one of the truly worthy combatants in Al Davis's career.

Len Dawson teamed with Otis Taylor, and Mike Garrett made runs when he needed to in Kansas City's 17–7 win. It was a bitter pill for Oakland to swallow. They had to watch Kansas City dismantle Minnesota 23–7 in Super Bowl IV. By 1970, the NFL was embarrassed. The AFL's superiority, so much of which had Al Davis's fingerprints all over it, was obvious. The merger benefited the senior league much more, giving them a chance to compete with the "big boys," instead of vice versa.

THE HEIDI GAME

On November 17, 1968, the New York Jets visited the Oakland–Alameda County Coliseum to play the Oakland Raiders. It was certainly a very important game for both teams, especially the Raiders. They were locked in a vicious battle for Western Division supremacy with the Kansas City Chiefs.

The game was nationally televised by NBC. Naturally, since it involved a New York team—a great, very popular New York team with a quarterback as popular as any rock star of the era—it promised huge TV ratings.

The game has been replayed countless times on NFL Films and ESPN Classic. It will forever be remembered as "The *Heidi* Game."

It was a classic AFL shootout, with the lead changing hands eight times. A full house swayed with the emotions of victory and defeat hovering in the air—desperately possible one minute, seemingly snatched away the next.

Two players who attended college in Utah played a major role in that game. Both were from the East Bay. Charlie Smith of the Raiders, while running track for Castlemont High of Oakland, defeated future Olympic gold medal champion Jim Hines of McClymonds. Smith, a 6′1″ running back at Utah, had been drafted by Oakland and was used in a fairly new manner. In the Raider scheme under Al Davis, a running back did not simply carry the ball and block; he was also a receiver. Smith was often the target of Lamonica's outlet passes.

The Jets had a place-kicker known as the "Crockett Rocket" because he hailed from nearby Crockett. Jim Turner played at Utah State. His 26-yard field goal put New York ahead 32–29 late in the game.

Turner kicked off to Smith, who returned it to the Raider 23. NBC cut to a commercial. It was 4:00 PM on the West Coast, 7:00 PM back east. Fans at the Coliseum were of course glued to their seats. All the Raiders needed to do was sustain a drive and set up a game-tying field goal, or maybe even a game-winning touchdown. With Lamonica at the controls and dangerous weapons at his disposal, such a possibility was not remote.

Blackout rules for home games meant Bay Area fans within 90 miles of Oakland did not view the game on their TVs, but around America fans were watching in the Central, Rocky Mountain, and Pacific time zones, and in L.A. and Sacramento. In New York and throughout the East Coast, where the game held fever interest,

BY THE NUMBERS

117—The single-season scoring record set by George Blanda in 1968.

fans watched the commercial, figuring that it would end and the game would resume.

Alas, NBC had a dilemma on its hands. That Sunday night at 7:00 PM the family classic *Heidi* was scheduled. This is the well-known story of a little Swiss girl who lives with her grandfather in the Alpine Mountains, a staple of wholesome entertainment. In the days before cable, pay-per-view, VHS, DVD, TiVo, record, rewind, and 700 channels—when the choices came down to what NBC, ABC, CBS, and maybe a handful of local stations wanted to show the public, TV viewers scheduled their days around events like *Heidi*. It was on once a year. If one missed it, they missed it until the next year.

"I WILL ALWAYS REMEMBER JOHNNY SAMPLE, WHO PLAYED CORNERBACK FOR THE JETS, COMING UP TO ME AND SAYING, 'NICE TRY, LAMONICA. BETTER LUCK NEXT YEAR.'"

—DARYLE LAMONICA

At the NBC offices in New York City, program executives judged their alternatives. Most pro football games had lasted three hours or less up until then. A game scheduled at 1:00 PM in Oakland would be over by 4:00, but the AFL was a new deal. All those passes, incompletions, first downs, chains moving, time-outs, guys going out of bounds...the game now lasted more than three hours, and this one surely did.

With the ball on the Oakland 23 and only 1:05 remaining, a quick decision had to be made based on what they knew. The Raiders really needed a win, not a tie, since they were deadlocked with Kansas City. Seventy-seven yards in a minute seemed to be a tall order. Lamonica and his teammates could not get it done. Could they?

Switch to *Heidi*. The commercial ended on the East Coast. Football fans at home and in bars suddenly saw an adorable little blonde girl hiking in the Swiss Alps. The reaction to her visage was less than adorable. The more adept fans found the radio to hear the closing minute, but this was not an option for many. Some returned from the bathroom, saw *Heidi*, and figured the clock had run out (a Jet victory) and that was that. Many had dinner waiting, parties to go to.

Many, of course, went ballistic. Calls flooded NBC's offices immediately. Savvy Jet fans *knew* what Lamonica and the Raiders could do with one minute on the clock, and this filled their hearts with dread.

Back in Oakland, Lamonica split the Jet seam with a pass to Smith, similar in some ways to Matt Leinart's pass to Dwayne Jarrett with 1:32 to go to propel USC's 2005 victory over Notre Dame. Smith raced to glory, giving Oakland the win...

Except that a flag nullified the play. The crowd groaned. In New York, Heidi's smile dared football fans to throw their shoes through the sets.

"I will always remember Johnny Sample, who played cornerback for the Jets, coming up to me and saying, 'Nice try, Lamonica. Better luck next year,'" the Raider QB said, as quoted in *The Oakland Raiders: Stadium Stories* by Tom LaMarre.

"IF FOOTBALL WASN'T OVER, WE WOULD STILL GO TO HEIDI AT 7:00 O'CLOCK. SO I WAITED AND I WAITED AND I HEARD NOTHING. WE CAME UP TO THAT MAGIC HOUR AND I THOUGHT, 'WELL, I HAVEN'T BEEN GIVEN ANY COUNTERORDER, SO I'VE GOT TO DO WHAT WE AGREED TO DO.'"

—DICK CLINE, NBC EXECUTIVE, ON WHY HE SWITCHED AWAY FROM THE END OF THE RAIDERS-JETS GAME TO AIR HEIDI

Not so fast. Lamonica hit Smith for 20. Jet safety Mike D'Amato (who replaced starter Jim Hudson, tossed out earlier for unsportsmanlike conduct) committed a face-mask penalty, putting the ball on the New York 43. The emotions were raw and edgy. It was that way whenever the Raiders played. The AFL in those days resembled trench warfare. With the clock stopped, Lamonica composed himself, called Smith's number, knowing D'Amato could not catch him, and completed a sideline touchdown pass to give Oakland the 36–32 lead.

"I would have outrun Hudson, too," Smith said. "The play that was called back was a circle pattern, but teams were getting wise to that. So on the touchdown, I ran to the hash mark on the right side and then broke to the sideline.

"That play was open all day, but Daryle told me to be patient, that we would get to it. Our wide receivers ran deep patterns to clear out the secondary, and then I just cut underneath."

DID YOU KNOW...

That the Raiders and Chiefs were both 12–2 in the 1968 regular season, forcing a playoff for the right to play the Jets in the AFL title game? The Raiders dismantled K.C. 41–6 at the Coliseum.

In New York, Heidi was getting scolded by her grandfather. The NBC switchboard literally blew a fuse. Fans screamed epithets at the little girl. But many figured the Jets had won, which was the reason the game was not on anymore. They went off into the Manhattan night confident of this.

It was still not over. Oakland kicked off, and New York's Earl Christy fumbled the ball. Preston Ridlehuber recovered the ball on th 2-yard line and ran it into the end zone. Oakland scored 14 points in nine seconds to win the game 43–32.

Jet coach Weeb Ewbank's wife, like many, assumed her man's team had won. She called the coach in the visitors' locker room and offered a hearty "Congratulations."

"What do you mean?" retorted Ewbank, thinking it a cruel joke. "We lost." He slammed the phone down. For those who went to the movies, attended dinner parties, and did other things assuming the Jets won, the 11:00 o'clock news, the next day's newspapers, and the water cooler chatter provided a shocking reversal of fortunes. Others, watching *Heidi*, were astounded when an NBC crawl ran across their screens with the words: "RAIDERS 43, JETS 32."

"[Prior to the game] it was determined that *Heidi* would air at 7:00 o'clock," said NBC broadcast operation supervisor Dick Cline, a man whose name lives in TV infamy. "If football wasn't over, we would still go to *Heidi* at 7:00 o'clock. So I waited and I waited and I heard nothing. We came up to that magic hour and I thought, 'Well, I haven't been given any counterorder, so I've got to do what we agreed to do."

FIGHTING MAD

When the Raiders and Jets played each other in 1968, feelings of rivalry bordering on hatred between the two teams existed. Oakland's Ben Davidson had broken Joe Namath's cheekbone the season before.

Cline, it turns out, was the victim of poor communications. With seven minutes remaining in what was obviously the game of the year, NBC officials (most of whom were Jets' frontrunners in 1968) watching at home called each other and agreed to air the game to its completion. They called Cline to tell him to delay *Heidi*. The problem was that thousands of fans were also calling NBC to find out whether the game or the girl would be on the air at 7:00. The switchboard was so full, none of the NBC execs could get through, so Cline never got the counterorder. There were no cell phones, no fax machines, no emails to override the busy signals.

"People began calling before 7:00 o'clock saying one of two things," said former NBC executive Chet Simmons. "'What are you going to do about *Heidi*?' Or, 'Don't let the game go on.' What it did was, it literally blew out the switchboard."

The game's aftermath created future TV contracts ensuring that visiting team's viewers would always see a game to its conclusion no matter what.

An hour and a half after the game, amid great uproar, NBC president Julian Goodman released a statement: "It was a forgivable error committed by humans who were concerned about children expecting to see *Heidi* at 7:00 PM. I missed the end of the game as much as anyone else."

Unable to call NBC, many fans called the New York Police Department, causing havoc and leading to front-page headlines in *The New York Times*.

"The *Heidi* Game" was later voted the most memorable regular-season game in history and one of the 10 most memorable ever in a 1997 poll.

KNOCKIN' ON THE DOOR OF GREATNESS

Ray Guy was drafted in the first round in 1973, a rare thing for a punter but a testament to his skills, which he utilized to the great benefit of his team over the years. It should land him in the Hall of Fame. For 14 years, Guy mastered the "coffin corner kick" and gave his team great field position time and time again.

Raymond Chester was traded to Baltimore for Bubba Smith. Smith, a monster defensive back from Michigan State, came out of Beaumont, Texas, to spur Duffy Daugherty's Spartans into the 1966 "Game of the Century" versus Note Dame, a memorable 10–10 tie at East Lansing.

Smith had gone to the Baltimore Colts, where he led Don Shula's team to a 13–1 record and the 1968 NFL championship, only to lose in ignominious fashion to "Broadway Joe" Namath and the "Super Jets."

Fans exhorted Smith to "Kill, Bubba, Kill," and he was a ferocious player—his size and strength being intimidating. But inside Bubba was the sensitive heart of a poet. Smith would go on to an acting career. His younger brother, Tody, played on the USC team that beat Alabama in the 1970 "tackling segregation" game at Birmingham. Tody had brought a gun with him, but for reasons spiritual as much as practical chose to put his fate "in God's hands," leaving the weapon in his bag instead of brandishing it at Legion Field in an act that would have caused a riot. Tody, through Bubba's Hollywood connections, was trying to make a movie about the game when he passed away in the 1990s.

> **TRIVIA**
>
> What was defensive back Skip Thomas's self-given nickname?
>
> Find the answers on page 177.

Perhaps Bubba's sensitivity prevented him from achieving the kind of all-time greatness he otherwise might have, despite his "Kill, Bubba, Kill" reputation. In '73 Oakland had a good, but not great, 9–4–1 record. They defeated Kansas City, a great team that suddenly seemed to have grown old at the worst time, just as they moved into their gleaming new Arrowhead Stadium. The '73

8 GAMES TO SAVOR

1. 1974: Raiders 28, Dolphins 26 (playoffs, "Sea of Hands")
2. 1970: Raiders 23, Browns 20 ("George Blanda is king of the world!")
3. 1968: Raiders 43, Jets 32 ("*Heidi* game")
4. 1970: Raiders 14, Jets 13 (Lamonica-to-Wells)
5. 1978: Raiders 21, Chargers 20 ("Holy Roller")
6. 1976: Raiders 24, Patriots 21 (playoffs, roughing the passer called on Pats)
7. 1981: Raiders 14, Browns 12 (playoffs, Davis intercepts Sipe in the ice)
8. 1984: Raiders 38, Redskins 9 (Super Bowl, Marcus Allen leads the way)

Raiders were one of those teams that, on any given Sunday could beat anybody in the league but seemed not to have found its consistent self. Ken Stabler, normally accurate to a tee, was intercepted an inordinate amount in 1973, which contributed to their below-par record.

The 1973 campaign began with what by now was a predictable, disturbing trend—a loss—this time in the form of a 24–16 disappointment at the hands of Minnesota. George Atkinson was their lone bright spot with a punt return for a touchdown.

But Oakland demonstrated the next week why they were so dangerous—maybe not the best team in pro football, but a team that could beat the best. The Dolphins came to town riding an 18-game winning streak but, in a defensive struggle, fell to Oakland 12–7. A scheduling conflict involving the world champion Oakland A's forced the Raiders into playing the game at Cal's Memorial Stadium, the field they had been denied from calling home back in 1960.

Oakland then took on Kansas City, their one-time hated rival who were experiencing down years (the club has never truly returned to the glory of the 1960s, in all the years since). Phil Villapiano made 11 unassisted tackles, but the vaunted Raider offense was no place to be found in the 16–3 loss. This was the turning point in Raider annals, when John Madden finally decided to cut loose from the commitment to Daryle Lamonica.

Age and sophisticated defensive schemes had taken their toll on "the Mad Bomber." Stabler was brought in. While he was intercepted too much in his first full year, he never relinquished the spot. The press began to focus on Kenny. The further they dug, the more nuggets they found. Snake was from L.A., as in Lower Alabama, what he called the "Redneck Riviera." He was a high livin' party animal, in-season or offseason.

The former Notre Damer Lamonica had been aloof, more concerned with his business investments than hangin' out with his teammates. Stabler, on the other hand, much like a later Oakland celebrity, Jason Giambi, became the "social director." He arranged for regular forays to various seedy Oakland bars, including legendary sessions at a lounge near the Oakland Airport. The press began to report on wild goings-on, and the Raider image—on top of Ben Davidson's motorcycle trips, Hunter Thompson's *Rolling Stone* story—was further burnished.

Oakland immediately began to respond to Stabler's unifying on- and off-field presence. Drinking and team play have never been associated with winning. No coach wants his players knocking themselves down with spirits. Yet somehow, some way, Snake and his teammates had the "right stuff," so to speak. Kenny was ready every Sunday, and in his first two efforts came away with 17–10 (St. Louis) and 27–17 (San Diego) victories. Stabler's 19-of-31 performance against the Cardinals was rare in an offense that was perennially used to the quarterback completing well under 50 percent of his low-percentage bombs.

Snake's ball-control style, mixed with the occasional long ball, revitalized Madden's offense, giving their running backs a chance to show what they could do, too. The San Diego game was a symbolic changing of the old guard, with 1960s superstars Lamonica and San Diego's Johnny Unitas watching from the bench while Snake and Dan Fouts squared off, the first of many confrontations.

On Monday night at Denver, Stabler was spectacular with his passing but not so much with his scrambling. Six sacks in a 23–23 tie offset his 313 yards in the air, but Snake may have had his greatest pure game the following week in Baltimore. He completed 25-of-29 passes for 304 yards. With help from Clarence Davis (32-yard TD run), the Raiders prevailed 34–21.

The New York Giants, a shell of their old selves, came to the Coliseum and were like lambs put to slaughter in a 42–0 Raider triumph. But two straight home games with Pittsburgh and Cleveland were a disaster.

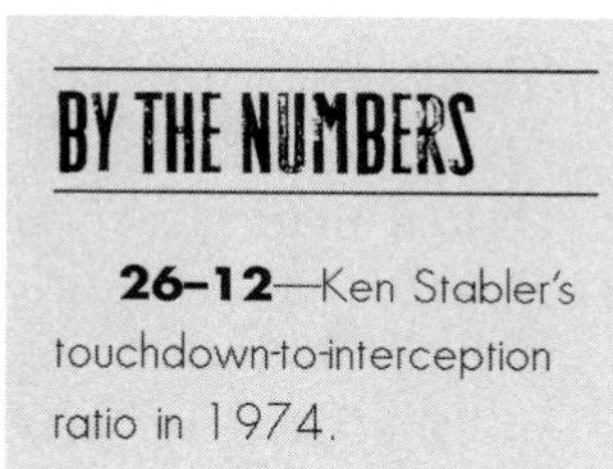

26–12—Ken Stabler's touchdown-to-interception ratio in 1974.

Stabler's minor injury partially explained how the team, which had been so potent, could suddenly be so inept. Of course, the great Steeler defense put the clamps on many a talented quarterback in the 1970s. In '73 they felled Stabler and the Silver and Black in an impressive 17–9 win. The carry-over effect was obvious when the Raiders lost to Cleveland the next week 7–3 in front of an Oakland crowd.

But the famed "pride and poise" of the Davis mystique showed itself in fine form when Oakland reeled off four straight wins to capture the Western Division. San Diego was no match, losing 31–3, with George Atkinson dominating his side of the ball.

At the Astrodome, Dan Pastorini was bottled up in Oakland's 17–6 win. Then it was payback time against the Chiefs, 37–7. Marv Hubbard rushed for 115 yards. Mike Siani, Charlie Smith, and Clarence Davis then keyed a tight 21–17 win over Denver to give Oakland the division championship and a shot in the playoffs.

The first round featured Oakland's burning desire for revenge, revenge, and more revenge, when the Steelers came to Oakland. This game marks the development of the rivalry—two of the three great AFC powers of the decade, not yet fully developed, and therefore neither quite ready to unseat Miami.

The repercussions of "the Immaculate Reception" were on everybody's mind, perhaps more so than beating Miami or getting to the Super Bowl. On this day, it was all Raiders. Stabler directed them masterfully, with Hubbard, Smith, and Davis dominating the turf with pounding runs to spur the 33–14 win. Willie Brown tortured Terry Bradshaw with a key interception that he returned 54 yards for an Oakland score.

The Raider offensive line was shaping up to become what history records is the greatest, or one of the greatest, ever assembled: Art Shell, Gene Upshaw, Jim Otto, George Buehler, and John Vella. The vaunted Steeler ground attack was limited to a mere 65 yards rushing. Blanda, not ready for retirement just yet, contributed four field goals.

The next great obstacle facing the Raiders was Miami. Like the Packers, Jets, and Chiefs of years past, they were too tough to overcome. Oakland played the great Dolphins competitively, but in the fourth quarter, Garo Yepremian kicked a field goal, and Larry Csonka scored a backbreaking touchdown to widen the final spread, 27–10.

The Dolphin offense of that era more closely resembled a college team of the Woody Hayes or Bo Schembechler variety. Even though quarterback Bob Griese had been a passing sensation at Purdue, and indeed was a Canton-worthy pro signal-caller, the Dolphin ground game was so devastating, and their defense so impregnable, that Don Shula chose an offensive approach that was almost more conservative than Ronald Reagan.

Mercury Morris and Csonka thundered away behind the blocking of Larry Little and Norm Evans. An interception in the fourth quarter also killed the Silver and Black. Miami rarely made those kinds of mistakes.

"JUST WIN, BABY!"

The Oakland Raiders went through a transition period in 1978 and 1979. In 1980 there was little sentiment favoring their chances at returning to the glory days. That was precisely what they did, however, in an improbable season surrounded by turmoil, which somehow seems to always be just the way Al Davis likes it. They did what the managing general partner simply asked of them: "Just win, baby!"

DID YOU KNOW...

That cornerback Lester Hayes was named Defensive Player of the Year in 1980?

John Madden retired from coaching. He claimed to have been stressed out, and did not like to fly. He has steadfastly maintained over the years he was not pushed out, nor did he leave over disagreements with the intrusive Davis.

Slowly but surely, many of the great stars of the 1970s became older, replaced by the many fine draft choices that now bore fruit. The most notable of these was Kenny Stabler, who performed erratically in his last two years in Oakland. He was traded to Houston, where he did have success before eventually calling it quits.

Dan Pastorini, a one-time wunderkind from the University of Santa Clara, was brought in, expected to lead the team, but in his pro career since the 1971 Draft he had not shown why this was a reasonable hope.

The same could be said of Jim Plunkett. Plunkett and Pastorini were part of the famed "Year of the Quarterback," collegiate seniors in 1970 who dominated the spring draft. Plunkett won the Heisman Trophy, leading Stanford to victory over Ohio State in the Rose Bowl. New England selected him first. Aside from Plunkett and Pastorini, 1970 senior quarterbacks included Joe Theismann of Notre Dame, Lynn Dickey of Kansas, and Archie Manning of Ole Miss.

Raider fans were nonplussed by the acquisition of Pastorini and Plunkett. Plunkett was considered completely over the hill, having failed in New England and disappointed in his return home to San Francisco.

Tom Flores replaced Madden in 1979. Fans would have preferred that *he* play quarterback, as he had so effectively in the 1960s. Pretty boys like Pastorini or ballyhooed collegiate superstars like Plunkett did not compare in their minds to a guy like Stabler, who played "ugly" but got the job done.

On top of these developments, Davis was mired in a controversy over the Oakland Coliseum, proposed luxury boxes, and courtship by the city of Los Angeles, which Davis made plainly obvious he took seriously.

Former USC star wide receiver Bob Chandler was acquired from Buffalo for Phil Villapiano. Biletnikoff either retired or was

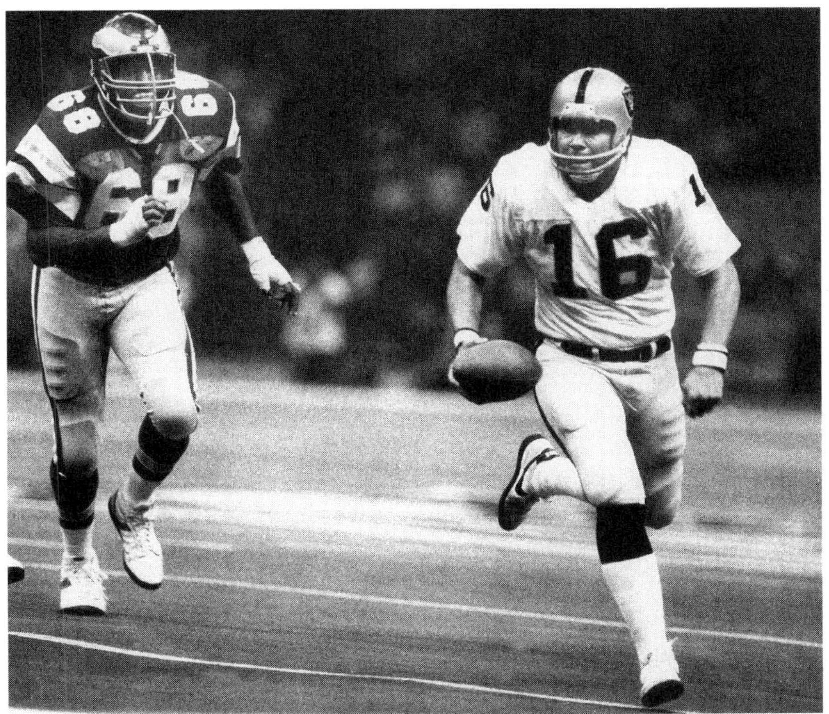

Quarterback Jim Plunkett was at his best in the postseason, twice leading the Raiders to NFL championships. Here he scrambles away from an Eagles defender during Oakland's 27–10 victory in Super Bowl XV; Plunkett was the game's MVP.

made to retire. Jack Tatum was gone, and Kenny King was in. Cedrick Hardman and Joe Campbell shored up the defensive line. Defensive back Odis McKinney came from the Giants, Dwayne O'Steen from the Rams. Kicker Chris Bahr replaced Jim Breech. Linebacker Matt Millen from Penn State would pay immediate dividends. BYU super QB Marc Wilson had some people thinking that he was the future.

Pastorini had led winning Oiler teams, but he'd had Earl Campbell to hand off to in Houston. He impressed nobody as the team lost three of its first five, but destiny played its hand when Pastorini was injured against San Diego, leading to the desperation move of Plunkett's calling signals. A few weeks later, Pastorini broke his leg, and again Plunkett was brought in.

San Diego, a powerhouse offense led by Dan Fouts, came to town. To everybody's surprise, most notably the Chargers, Plunkett was effective, and the defense applied pressure in stopping Fouts in a 38–24 win. When the Raiders won on Monday night the following week against Pittsburgh, 45–34, it was impossible not to be impressed by the improvement.

Plunkett, Chandler, Morris Bradshaw, Rod Martin—they all performed well, as did veteran Cliff Branch. Plunkett was again terrific in a 33–14 win over Seattle, hitting Chandler for three scores while Lester Hayes wreaked havoc in the defensive secondary. The line recorded six sacks.

Miami fell 16–10. Despite three fumbles, Oakland prevailed over Cincinnati, 28–17. Arthur Whittington's 90-yard kickoff return keyed a 19–17 win over the Seahawks. With a six-game winning streak, Oakland traveled to Veterans Stadium to take on the "best" team in pro football, the Philadelphia Eagles of quarterback Ron "the Polish Rifle" Jaworski and coach Dick Vermeil. Despite losing 10–7, the game demonstrated that, if they could get to the postseason, they might prevail.

With the defense now firing on all cylinders, they beat Denver 9–3, with Plunkett scoring the only TD. But Dallas beat Oakland 19–13. Chandler scored two touchdowns in beating Denver 24–19, and in the final week they wrapped up an 11–5 wild-card berth with a big victory over the Giants.

Houston entered the Coliseum, and it was old home week, with Stabler, Tatum, and Dave Casper suited up for Bum Phillips's Oilers. The Raider defense sacked Snake seven times, and Earl Campbell was shut down, while Plunkett hit Whittington and Todd Christensen with TD passes in a stirring 27–7 win.

Next came one for the ages, when the warm-weather Californians traveled to Cleveland for a game on frozen, windswept Lake Erie in January. Playing on virtual ice, brutal conditions, the Raiders tightened up on defense in minus 16 degrees. Lester Hayes dominated in the secondary, as was his custom.

Mark van Eeghen bullrushed in for a score to give Oakland a slim 14–12 lead in the fourth quarter, but Cleveland was driving. Quarterback Brian Sipe just needed a field goal, but the blustery conditions made that less than a sure thing. He risked a touchdown pass and paid the ultimate price when Mike Davis intercepted the ball in front of Ozzie Newsome to give Oakland the win.

TRIVIA

What three Raiders have been named Most Valuable Player in the Super Bowl?

Find the answers on page 177.

Overcoming the harrowing Cleveland conditions gave the Raiders a sense of freedom, and playing for the title on the sun-swept plains of San Diego Stadium seemed a walk in the park afterward. Of course, stopping Dan Fouts would be a challenge for the ages. He was not actually "stopped," but neither was Plunkett in the wide-open affair.

Oakland got lucky when Plunkett's deflected pass was caught by Ray Chester for a 65-yard score. King and van Eeghen scored TDs, but with a 34–27 lead in the fourth quarter, Fouts loomed dangerously on the Charger sideline. In a magnificent showing, van Eeghen and King ground out first down after first down in a seven-minute drive to clinch the game and send Al Davis and his men to the Super Bowl, where Philadelphia awaited.

The game was played in New Orleans, one of America's great party towns. Vermeil kept a tight lid on the Eagles, as if they were in stir, waiting out the days in their swank hotel rooms. Despite Stabler's departure, the Raiders were as frolicking as ever, hitting Bourbon Street with the enthusiasm of frat boys during Rush Week. John Matuszak was spotted dancing with a young lovely the night before the game, but in typical Raider style, neither Davis, Flores, nor anybody else complained, so long as he performed on Sunday, which he did.

It was not even close. Oakland dominated the first half, with Rod Martin's interception setting up a Branch touchdown. Jaworski was stymied while Plunkett hit King on a beautiful 80-yard sideline scamper to give the Raiders a 14–3 lead at the midway point.

Martin intercepted two more Jaworski passes, and Plunkett finished with 13 completions on 21 attempts for 261 yards, winning the MVP award and the Super Bowl, 27–10.

AMAZING GRACE

Jim Plunkett's life story reads like a Dickens novel—or a combination of them. Throw in *Bleak House* and *Great Expectations*, then *A Tale of Two Cities*, with a happy ending like *A Christmas Carol*. He always had an unassuming personality, yet he rode the whirlwind of drama wherever he went.

There is a saying, which Richard Nixon always liked to quote, that started off, "Nothing in the world can take the place of persistence. Talent alone cannot. There is nothing more common in the world than unsuccessful men with talent."

This is a true statement, and words to live by. The Horatio Alger message of these inspirational words is the driving force behind most successful people in all walks of life. It certainly is reflected in the life and career of Jim Plunkett.

Plunkett grew up poor in San Jose. His Mexican-American parents were both blind.

"I was even embarrassed about where and how we lived in San Jose," Plunkett wrote in *The Jim Plunkett Story*. "Eventually I outgrew my embarrassment. I came to the conclusion that if you love someone, what difference does it make how much money is in the family bank account?"

Plunkett was the star quarterback at James Lick High School, but not a national blue chipper. He was recruited locally and by UCLA, but not by USC. Ironically, they recruited Mike Holmgren, then a more-celebrated quarterback from Lincoln High in San Francisco. Ultimately, he was not Plunkett's equal, although he did win a Super Bowl coaching at Green Bay.

Plunkett earned a scholarship to prestigious Stanford University, which was only a few miles north on the 101 Freeway, but a world apart from what he was used to. Plunkett's father passed away after his first year at Stanford, creating further obstacles to overcome.

"I was a poor, shy Mexican kid from east San Jose trying to mingle with the confident, intelligent scions of wealth who attend Stanford," Plunkett wrote. "Many times I thought to myself: 'Maybe, Jim, you belong someplace else.'"

SCANDAL

After Ken Stabler posed in the nude with topless dancer Carol Doda, and Dan Pastorini appeared in *Playgirl*, what did Jim Plunkett do? He won two Super Bowls and, in answer to whether he would appear in similar magazine layouts, asked, "Who would want to look at me?"

On top of that, coach John Ralston was unimpressed with Plunkett's quarterbacking skills, suggesting that he switch to defensive end.

"I want to play quarterback," Plunkett told Ralston. "Tell me what I have to do."

Ralston gave Plunkett a summer regimen to follow, knowing that he would either take to the challenge or fall by the wayside.

"When he came back in the fall, you wouldn't have believed the difference," said Ralston.

With the help of assistant coach Dick Vermeil, Plunkett learned how to throw on the run, a key in Ralston's play-action schemes. While the more ballyhooed Mike Holmgren sat on the Southern California bench, Plunkett beat out all the competition to assume Stanford's starting spot in his redshirt sophomore season. He never looked back.

In 1968, Plunkett led Stanford to a 20–0 victory over Cal in the Big Game at Berkeley, establishing himself as one of the nation's best signal-callers. In 1969, he continued to revitalize the once-moribund Stanford Indians football program, and would have had his team in the Rose Bowl except for a last-second USC field goal, denying them a trip to Pasadena.

In 1970, Plunkett entered the season in the discussion for All-America and Heisman Trophy honors. He was not the favorite, however. Archie Manning of Mississippi and Joe Theismann of Notre Dame (who actually changed pronunciation of his name from *Thees*-man to *Thys*-man as part of the school's marketing campaign) were considered the more likely prospects.

In the fifth game of the season, Plunkett elevated himself into the favorite's role by engineering a brilliant 24–14 victory over the

During eight years with the Patriots and 49ers, Jim Plunkett failed to live up to the promise that earned him a Heisman Trophy in college. Oakland picked him up as a backup, and in 1980 he came off the Raiders' bench and led the team to a Super Bowl championship.

mighty Trojans. After following that with a 63–16 demolishing of Washington State, Stanford was in the driver's seat for the Rose Bowl, too.

Victories over UCLA and Washington clinched it. Theismann was brilliant in a driving rainstorm against USC at the L.A. Coliseum, but his team lost the game 38–28, which probably gave Plunkett just enough to win the Heisman in a regional vote. Then the Indians took on the unbeaten Ohio State Buckeyes. This was said to be Woody Hayes's greatest team, led by quarterback Rex Kern and safety Jack Tatum. The "sure thing" victory over Stanford would give them their second national title in three years.

TRIVIA

How many Heisman Trophy winners have played for the Raiders?

Find the answers on page 177.

Instead, Plunkett was marvelous, hitting receiver Randy Vataha just before a blitzing Tatum could get to him. The touchdown sealed Stanford's 27–17 win, considered one of the greatest upsets in Rose Bowl history.

Plunkett was riding high. Drafted number one in 1971, he beat Oakland 20–6, in his pro debut at Foxboro Stadium. That was his last hurrah—until taking over the Raiders in 1980.

"The biggest problem was that Jim was billed as The Franchise from the start," said Vataha, who teamed up with him in New England, as well. "People believed that, especially after his first year. The next two years were bad years. It soon became that everything that happened to the Patriots, good or bad, was attributed to Jim."

After the drafting of Alabama offensive lineman John Hannah and USC fullback Sam "Bam" Cunningham in 1973, the Pats improved, but by the mid-1970s the team had lost faith in Plunkett. Worse, Plunkett seemed to have lost faith in himself. Steve Grogan became New England's starter, and Plunkett eventually found himself in San Francisco.

It was supposed to be so perfect: the Bay Area product and Stanford star coming home—another John Brodie, it was felt—but the 49ers were terrible. This was aggravated by the fact that the cross-bay Raiders were a 1970s dynasty. Plunkett quickly learned that his Stanford heroics were long forgotten.

"Booing, I learned to my chagrin," he said, "is a national and not a regional affliction."

Plunkett never did join up with another San Francisco native, O.J. Simpson, who joined the team in 1978. O.J. was legitimately past his prime, and it certainly looked like Plunkett was, too, except that in his case he had never had a prime in pro football. Then the Raiders picked him up when nobody else wanted him, in 1978.

"It's all over," Plunkett told his old Stanford pal, Bob Moore, who had been cut by Tampa Bay himself. "I've got to think about doing something else."

But Al Davis saw something in Plunkett.

"Al Davis works with a Pygmalion syndrome," said Plunkett's attorney, Wayne Hooper. "He takes players who haven't made it elsewhere, for whatever reasons, but who have the ability. Then he rehabilitates them."

"I never wanted to play for the Raiders," said Plunkett. "I never even liked them. The 49ers were my team. The Raiders dressed in black, the Hell's Angels of football."

It was a miracle that Plunkett stuck around long enough to find success in Oakland. He sat behind Kenny Stabler in 1978 and 1979, but Wayne Hooper had predicted that Stabler would be traded at some point, which he was prior to 1980. An intelligent guy who graduated from Stanford with a B average, Plunkett had many options, but he refused to quit. Not when Stabler started. Not when Dan Pastorini was acquired and named the starter.

DID YOU KNOW...

That the Raiders' move to Los Angeles brought to a boil the legal troubles with the NFL and the personal feud between Pete Rozelle and Al Davis? Prior to the 1983 season, the Raiders added salt in the wound by winning a $35 million antitrust suit against the NFL for blocking the move to Los Angeles.

Finally, after Pastorini's 1980 injury, Plunkett got his opportunity and he made the most of it, leading the team to an 11–5 record, a wild-card berth, victory over Stabler and Houston, and then the trip to Cleveland in January of 1981.

"I was never as cold as I was January 4, 1981," he wrote.

The California native toughed it out, ironically beating out another Californian, San Diego State graduate Brian Sipe of the Browns. Then, in the San Diego sunshine the following week, he outdueled Dan Fouts of San Francisco's St. Ignatius High School.

"Jim Plunkett's comeback is one of the greatest stories in sports," said Tom Flores.

After beating still another more-heralded quarterback, "the Polish Rifle" Ron Jaworski and Philadelphia in the 1981 Super Bowl, Plunkett reflected on his career.

"I was lost for a while, almost forgotten," he wrote. "I could have quit and never made it, but I stuck it out."

In the music reel of Jim Plunkett's life, one hears the tender lyrics of "Amazing Grace...how sweet the sound."

RICH GANNON AND THE 2002 SUPER BOWL TEAM

The Raiders signed wide receiver Jerry Rice, who holds every major career receiving record, and he joined forces with all-time Raider great Tim Brown in the 1,000-yard club as the Raiders got off to a terrific start, winning eight of their first 10 games in 2001. The Raiders quickly overcame a stunning home loss to the Arizona Cardinals to clinch the division early with a 10–3 record. However, with home-field advantage up in the air, the Raiders coasted through their last three games, losing each. They were forced to play in the wild-card round after a 10–6 season.

In the wild-card game, Jerry Rice showed he was not done yet, collecting almost 200 receiving yards in an exciting 38–24 win over the New York Jets in Oakland. A week later, the Raiders appeared to be heading for the AFC Championship Game with a 13–10 win over the Patriots in the New England snow, as they scooped up a Tom Brady fumble with less then two minutes left. However, the play was reversed by instant replay thanks to the

Rich Gannon, like Jim Plunkett, was an underappreciated quarterback who blossomed late in his career with the Raiders. In 2002, Gannon had an MVP season and led Oakland to Super Bowl XXXVII, where they lost to Tampa Bay. An injury ended Gannon's career less than two years later.

obscure and controversial "tuck" rule. The Pats would go on to tie the game and take the opening drive in overtime deep into Raider territory, where they nailed a game-winning field goal to pull out a controversial 16–13 win. Following the season, coach Jon Gruden was *traded* to the Tampa Bay Buccaneers for draft picks after the team was unable to sign him to a contract extension. The reason no contract extension was reached was that Al Davis felt Gruden was stealing his spotlight. He wanted to reclaim some of the control Gruden had taken away from him in recent years. The Raiders would go on to name Bill Callahan to replace him.

Under Callahan, the Raiders came flying out of the gate, winning behind a high-powered offense that scored 162 points in their first four games. However, the Raiders suddenly went into a tailspin, losing four straight games. However, just as suddenly, the Raiders rebounded as Jerry Rice collected his 200th career touchdown in a 34–10 *Monday Night Football* road win over the Denver Broncos. The Monday night win started a five-game winning streak, including another Raider receiver having a "Monday night milestone."

TOP 10

Quarterback Comebacks (quarterbacks given up on by other teams that led new clubs to Super Bowls)

1. **Jim Plunkett, Raiders (1980, 1983)**
2. Earl Morrall, Colts (1968), Dolphins (1972)
3. Doug Williams, Redskins (1987)
4. Craig Morton, Broncos (1977)
5. **Rich Gannon, Raiders (2002)**
6. Joe Kapp, Vikings (1969)
7. Billy Kilmer, Redskins (1972)
8. Brett Favre, Packers (1996, 1997)
9. Trent Dilfer, Ravens (2000)
10. Len Dawson, Chiefs (1966, 1969)

Tim Brown became just the third wide receiver in NFL history to collect 1,000 career receptions, joining Rice and Cris Carter as the Raiders beat the New York Jets at home 26–20. After a loss to the Miami Dolphins on the road, the Raiders won the AFC West with a solid 11–5 record. Rich Gannon was named MVP, passing for 4,689 yards, while throwing 26 TD passes to just 10 interceptions. The Raiders earned home-field advantage in the AFC, facing the Jets again in the division round. Tied at the half 10–10, the Raiders pulled away in the final quarter. Wide receiver Jerry Porter outshined his two future Hall of Fame teammates with 123 receiving yards, including a 50-yard reception that set up the game-breaking TD.

Hosting the Tennessee Titans in the AFC Championship Game, the veteran Raiders trailed 17–14 entering the final minutes of the first half. Suddenly, they caught a break, recovering a fumbled punt on the Titans' 16 to set up Rich Gannon's scoring strike. On the ensuing kickoff, the Raiders recovered another fumble to set up Sebastian Janikowski's field goal, giving them a 24–17 halftime lead. In the second half, the Raiders dominated the Titans to win 41–24, sending them to their first Super Bowl in 19 years.

Super Bowl week was described as the "Chucky Circus." The Raiders faced the Tampa Bay Buccaneers, coached by ex-Raider coach Jon Gruden. His visage has been described as resembling the "Chucky" character from a series of comic horror movies featuring an evil doll named Chucky.

Gruden, who coached the Raiders from 1998 to 2001, had built Oakland into a scoring machine that his replacement, Bill Callahan, helped form into the top offense in the NFL. They were matched up against Gruden's Buccaneers with the top defense in the NFL. The circus atmosphere overwhelmed Raider center Barret Robbins, who went AWOL the day before the big game in San Diego. Robbins reappeared the morning of the game after a night of drinking in Tijuana. He was suspended from the team, eventually determined to have a severe bipolar disorder that has negatively affected every aspect of his life in the succeeding years.

At the start of the game, it appeared as if the Robbins distraction would not hurt. The Raiders took advantage of an interception on the first possession of the game to take an early 3–0 lead. However, the Bucs' defense seemed to know what was coming. They read Rich Gannon perfectly, intercepting two passes, and shut down the Raider offense completely to take a 20–3 lead at the half. Things would not get better for the Raiders in the second half. Tampa Bay extended their lead to 27–3 on a long drive that ate up time in the third quarter. Gannon desperately attempted to get the Raiders back into the game but was picked off by Dwight Smith, who returned it all the way to extend their lead to 34–3. The Raiders made a furious attempt at a comeback, desperately trying to make a game of it, but in the final two minutes, Gannon had another two interceptions run back for touchdowns. The Buccaneers won the Super Bowl 48–21.

The man who led the new Raiders to the edge of the Promised Land, Rich Gannon, grew up in Philadelphia in the 1960s and '70s. He has two passions: "athletics and automobiles," according to writer Ken Hall. He was able to parlay football into a career that included one NFL MVP award (in 2002) and consecutive Pro Bowl MVP awards (in 2000 and 2001). Through the money he made in football, he was able to purchase a vintage car collection and, later, a "petroliana" collection.

DID YOU KNOW...

That famous actor Carl Weathers, who played Apollo Creed in three *Rocky* movies, also played linebacker for the Raiders in 1970 and 1971, after coming out of San Diego State University?

Petroliana, according to Hall, means "gas station collectibles, and it's a rapidly burgeoning genre." Gannon owns examples of authentic gas station memorabilia from a bygone era.

"After my rookie year [with the Minnesota Vikings in 1987], I went back to Philadelphia and bought a 1960 Buick Electra 225 convertible for $4,400," Gannon recalled. "My brother and I spent two years restoring it, doing the paint, interior, the motor, new top, new tires—the works. I still have that car today"—along with about a half-dozen others, although he's owned as many as 13 at a time.

Gannon attended St. Joseph's Prep School in Philadelphia, where he excelled in athletics. He attended the University of Delaware on a football scholarship and was selected in the fourth round (98th overall) of the 1987 NFL Draft by the New England Patriots. He was soon traded to the Minnesota Vikings, where he played sparingly for two seasons before breaking out in 1990.

That year, he became the Vikings' starting quarterback, displacing incumbent Wade Wilson. In 1993, he was traded to the Washington Redskins. Two years later, he was traded again, to the

IF ONLY...

Todd Marinovich, whom the Raiders chose with their first pick of the 1991 Draft, had not been such a bust, Al Davis probably would have chosen USC Heisman winner Matt Leinart in 2006. Speculation was that he was unwilling to be disappointed by two left-handed QBs from the same school.

Kansas City Chiefs. For two years he was a backup to Steve Bono. In 1997, he excelled as a starter but split duties with Elvis Grbac. In that year's playoffs, the team lost a close 14–10 contest to the Broncos.

In February 1999, the Raiders signed Gannon as a free agent, where he thrived under Gruden's West Coast offense. He was voted to the Pro Bowl four consecutive years. His greatest year was 2002, as he led Oakland to Super Bowl XXXVII. He led the league in pass attempts (with 618) and completions (418, a record). A shoulder injury cut short his 2003 season, while a serious neck injury in 2004 effectively ended his career. In 2005, Gannon retired from football to become an NFL analyst for CBS Sports.

WINNERS

UPSHAW

Gene Upshaw came to the Oakland Raiders as their first pick in the 1967 Draft out of tiny Texas A&I. Al Davis knew that there was a tremendous amount of hidden talent in those small schools, particularly in the South. The best pro football teams of the 1960s were the ones picking off these nuggets. The Raiders were one of the best pro football teams of the 1960s.

The 6′5″, 255-pounder was only the second guard ever inducted into Canton (1987). He was All-Pro or All-Conference 11 times, played in six Pro Bowls, and one AFL All-Star Game. He is the all-time Raider leader in games played with 217, having missed only one game in his career. He played in 207 straight games, playing in the Super Bowl in three decades (1968, 1977, and 1981). He holds the club record for playoff games (24), and was the offensive team captain from 1973 to 1981. In 15 years, Upshaw was the heart and soul of the greatest Raider teams of all time (11 playoff appearances, nine division titles, one AFL, two AFC, and two Super Bowl championships). He was named to the AFL-NFL 25-Year All-Star Team when the NFL held its 75th anniversary. He was also selected to the All–Monday Night Team, was a Hall of Famer on the first ballot, and became the executive director of the NFL Player's Association.

Upshaw had the gruff outward demeanor of an inmate from the original *Longest Yard,* but in truth he was a humorous man with an infectious laugh. His leadership skills and reputation for honesty were the things that led people to him, ultimately earning him the captaincy of the Raiders and later the directorship of the union.

Upshaw was always known as a helpful sort, and a true coach's dream. Madden always felt that if Upshaw was complaining, there was a valid problem that needed to be addressed. Upshaw's roommate in Oakland was Bob Brown, one of the best offensive tackles of his day.

"Gene, you're still just a kid," Brown told Upshaw, back when he was just a kid. "Wait until you've been around this game a while."

"I know what he wants to do," Upshaw said of Brown's prodding. "He wants to push me to the point where I give every ounce I have. Every player gets to the raging point. He needs somebody to give him a boost. Brown is my man."

When he was playing, Upshaw made it a point to speak to underprivileged kids, trying to steer them away from crime, drugs, and gang life. According to ex–San Francisco *Examiner* sportswriter Wells Twombly, who wrote *Oakland's Raiders: Fireworks and Fury*, Upshaw did not merely speak to the groups but actually visited the homes of wayward youth, getting involved in their lives, and trying to help.

"They tell me about their loneliness, their family problems, their troubles at school," Upshaw told Twombly in 1973. "Things that turn kids on drugs might not be a big thing to some people, but they're plenty big to these kids. Everybody takes love for granted. Lack of it can destroy a youngster. He hits the streets and pretty soon it's all over. I talked to a kid just the other day. He was on the streets looking for a love substitute. He found a pusher, instead. He's hooked."

"Upshaw...was a breakthrough-type guard," wrote Bob Carroll in *When the Grass Was Real*. "Offensive guards needed size, but they also had to be fast enough to lead sweeps. Most of them were around 6′2″ and 240 pounds; Gene was 6′5″ and 255, bigger than some offensive tackles, but still one of the quickest linemen in the league. From the time the Chiefs unveiled their giant defensive

Guard Eugene Upshaw was a devastating blocker, who is acknowledged as one of the greatest offensive lineman of all time. He played 16 years for the Raiders. Today, as executive director of the NFL Players Association, he remains one of the most powerful men in pro football.

tackle, Buck Buchanan, Al Davis began looking for a guard with Upshaw's combination of size and speed."

"I figured if Buchanan was going to play for the Chiefs for the next 10 years," said Davis, "we better get some big guy who can handle him. Those two guys put on some stirring battles over the years."

"I don't have as much fun pass blocking, but I get satisfaction from it," Upshaw said of the Raiders' dominant offensive scheme.

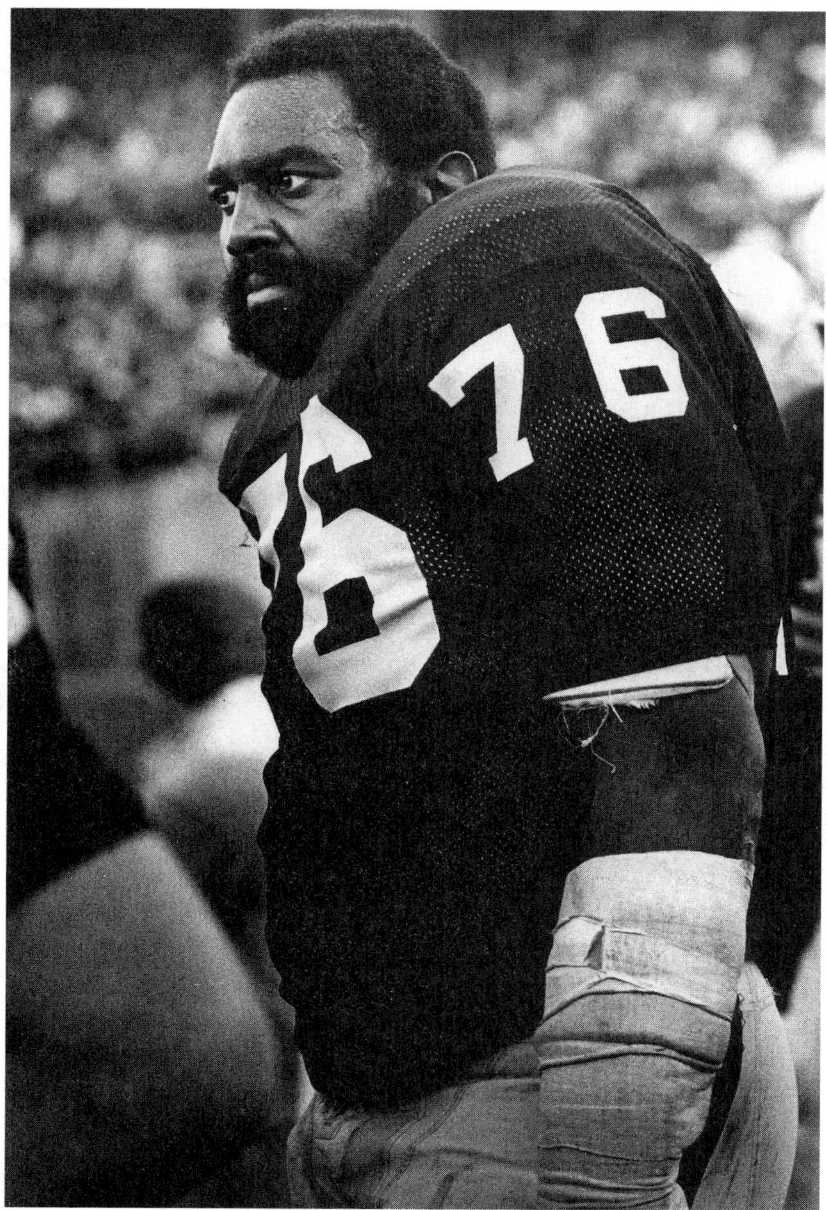

Massive offensive tackle Bob "Boomer" Brown was one of the largest football players of his era. His 10-year Hall of Fame career included stints with three different teams, but he spent his final three years, 1971–1973, with the Raiders.

"That's where we separate the men from the boys. It takes a hell of a man to stand in there on pass protection, to take those roundhouse clubs to the head and the butting with the helmets and all that. You've got to keep control of yourself.

"The good protection blocker sits and waits for the defense to make the move and then reacts. You have to be passive and aggressive at the same time. If you charge too hard, some of the quick linemen will get you off balance and skip around you or grab you and throw you. Or you might fire off at the wrong guy and the defense will be in a stunt and another guy will have an open road to your quarterback."

Upshaw specialized in running sweeps.

"That's my play," he said. "A wide receiver wants to catch a long touchdown pass. A defensive lineman wants to break in to sack a quarterback. I get my satisfaction pulling to lead those sweeps. That's a play where it comes down to just me and the defensive back. If I get him clean, we're going to make a long gain. If I miss him, we don't get a yard.

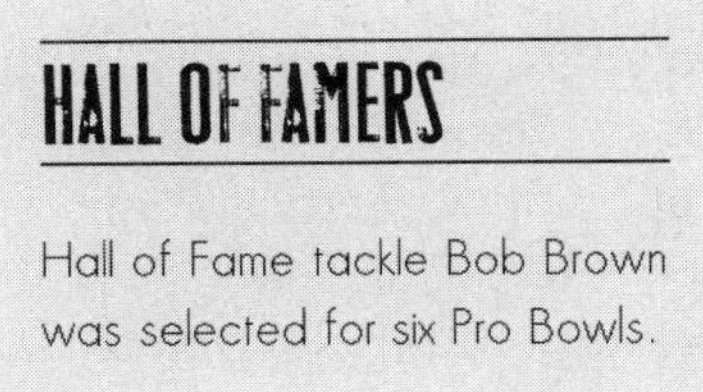

HALL OF FAMERS

Hall of Fame tackle Bob Brown was selected for six Pro Bowls.

"I'm weighing in at 260, coming right at that defensive back. He's 210 at most and 185 some of the time. And he hasn't got a chance. I've got it in my head that whatever he does has to be wrong. If he goes outside, I'm going to put him out of bounds. If he goes inside, I'll knock him in. And if he stands there, man, I'm going right over him."

Upshaw stayed in football—more or less—but not in the way one might have expected. He is to this day head of the players' union.

FLORES AND SHELL

Tom Flores and Art Shell are unique members of the Raider family. Both were star players, both became head coaches, and both are considered loyal to Al Davis, who prioritizes that as the ultimate Raider quality.

BUSINESS COMES FIRST

John Madden installed defensive changes in 1976. Some old pros were left "out in the cold," while some young ones found opportunity. It worked when the Raiders finally won a Super Bowl. Madden went from the traditional 4–3 to a 3–4 scheme, getting away from down linemen to an "Orange" defense. The key to its success was 6'2", 225-pound linebacker Willie Hall out of USC, who had previously been cut by Oakland. Also, Fred Steinfort beat out George Blanda for the kicker position in 1976 training camp, which led to Blanda's retirement. Jim Otto was retired by then, too, meaning two of their most venerable legends were not part of the Super Bowl championship team.

Flores was born on March 21, 1937, in Fresno, California. After graduating from the University of the Pacific in 1958, it took two years for Flores to make a professional football team. He was cut by the Calgary Stampeders of the Canadian Football League in 1958 and by the NFL's Washington Redskins in 1959.

When the AFL was established in 1960, Flores caught on with the Oakland Raiders. He became the team's starting quarterback early in the season, leading the league by completing 54 percent of his passes, throwing for 1,738 yards and 12 touchdowns.

Flores had his most productive season in 1966. Although he completed only 49.3 percent of his attempts, he passed for 2,638 yards and 24 touchdowns in 14 games.

Oakland traded him to the Buffalo Bills in 1967. A backup with Buffalo, Flores was released early in the 1969 season, then picked up by the Kansas City Chiefs. He spent the 1970 season on Kansas City's taxi squad, then retired as a player.

After serving as an assistant coach with Buffalo and Oakland, Flores took over as head coach of the Raiders in 1979. The franchise moved to Los Angeles in 1982. In nine seasons, he directed the Raiders to three first-place division finishes and Super Bowl victories after the 1980 and 1983 seasons.

While John Madden is often portrayed as the "face" of the Raiders, he has become more of a national television figure while

Flores remains the man who played, coached, worked in the front office, and broadcast for the Raiders. It is Flores, not Madden, who won not one but two Super Bowls.

While the 1976 team is generally accepted as the greatest in team history, and indeed one of the finest pro football teams ever assembled, 1983 in many ways marks the highest mountaintop scaled by the franchise. Playing in Los Angeles, where they were consolidating their fan base and new identity, the Raiders under Flores were a dominant team. Unlike 1977, when victory came over an overwhelmed Minnesota club, the January 1984 Super Bowl win came over a truly great Redskin team.

"We knew we had a good team," said Flores. "All the pieces were in place. But we didn't have Gene Upshaw and Art Shell for the first time in about 15 years, and we had to replace that leadership. But we felt we had enough veterans who would step forward.

"There are ups and downs in every championship season, and we didn't kill everybody we played that year, but we won some games in the fourth quarter. Great teams do that."

Jim Plunkett, in particular, blossomed—after years of floundering—under Flores's leadership. He was 35 in 1983 and had endured every kind of professional adversity while forging eventual success.

"We knew we could win with Plunkett because he had done it for us before, and we felt he still had something left," Flores said of the decision to stay with Plunkett instead of going to Marc Wilson. "But we also felt we could win with Wilson if we had to turn to him."

Flores was faced with his share of challenges in 1983, mainly in the form of Marcus Allen's early-season injury. In the 37–35 loss

BY THE NUMBERS

21—Raider playoff appearances (1967–1970, 1972–1977, 1980, 1982–1985, 1990–1991, 1993, 2000–2002).

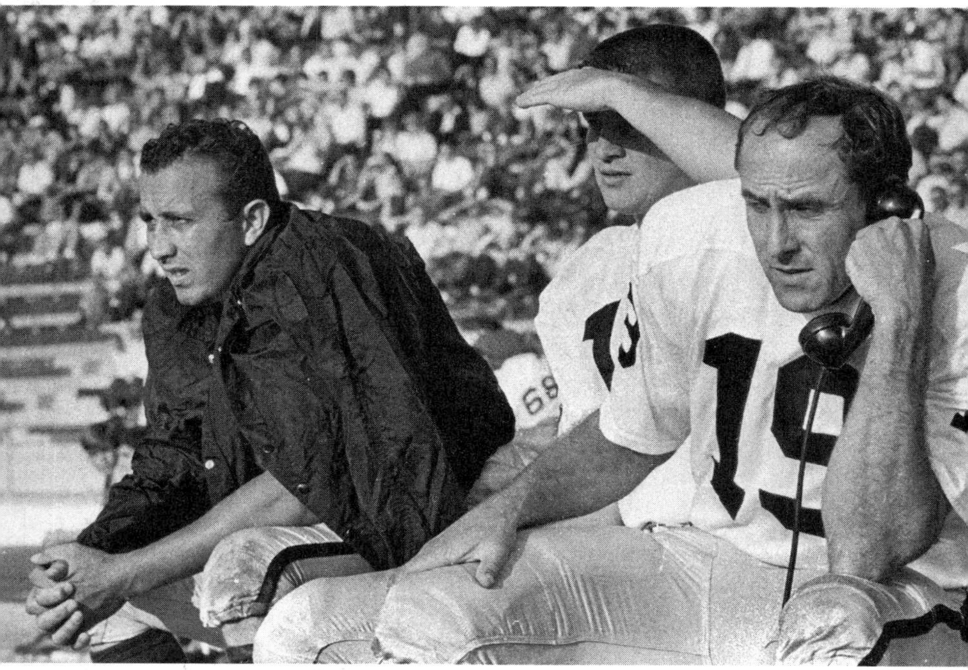

Backup Tom Flores (wearing jacket on the bench; Cotton Davidson is on the phone) would eventually get his chance to lead Oakland—first as starting quarterback and later as head coach. During his nine seasons as head coach, Flores led the Raiders to two Super Bowl wins.

to Washington during the regular season, Allen was unavailable, but Plunkett showed what he was made of. He threw four touchdown passes, rallying the team from a 13-point deficit to a 35–20 lead in the rollercoaster affair, before Joe Theismann led Washington to their ultimate comeback.

In 1988, Flores moved into the team's front office. After a year, he left to become president and general manager of the Seattle Seahawks. He named himself head coach in 1992, but was fired from both positions after the 1994 season.

As a player, Flores completed 838 of 1,715 passes for 11,959 yards and 92 touchdowns. He also rushed for five touchdowns. As a coach, he had a 97–87 record.

After the Raiders returned to Oakland, Flores joined the broadcasting team, sharing the booth with Greg Papa. He has remained a steadfast Raider, not playing the role of critic. Flores has avoided bad-mouthing his successors, although ultimately none of them have really approached where he took the franchise.

Art Shell joined the Raiders as a third-round draft choice in 1968, playing 15 years before induction into Pro Football's Hall of Fame on August 5, 1989. He was an All–American Football Conference selection six straight years, from 1973 to 1978, and an All-Pro in 1973, 1974, and 1977. Shell played in 207 league games, third-highest in the history of the Silver and Black.

He was selected to play in eight Pro Bowls, the most of any Raider player until wide receiver Tim Brown was selected to a ninth in 2001. Shell's career spanned three decades and included 23 postseason contests, including eight AFL-AFC championships and Raider victories in Super Bowls XI and XV. He was particularly credited with a near-perfect performance in the victory over Minnesota, limiting the Vikings' highly regarded defensive end Jim Marshall to no tackles, sacks, or assists during the 32–14 win.

He played in his first 156 games before missing five games due to a preseason injury, then launched into another streak of 51 straight games. Shell was named to the NFL All–Monday Night Team.

Shell came to Oakland after a stellar career as a two-way lineman at Maryland State–Eastern Shore. After retirement, he became the Raiders' offensive line coach until 1988, when he became head coach of the Silver and Black. He served as the head coach of the Raiders until 1994. Shell was later rehired after Bill Callahan's firing following the 2005 season.

THE REAL WILLIE BROWN

Willie Brown is not Willie Brown, Willie Brown, Willie Davis, or Willie Davis. Willie Brown of the Oakland Raiders is not Willie Brown, one-time "Ayatollah of the California Assembly" and mayor of San Francisco. He is not the Willie Brown who captained USC to the 1962 national championship, played in the NFL, and then became an assistant under John McKay.

He is not Willie Davis of the Green Bay Packers, or Willie Davis of the Los Angeles Dodgers.

For that matter, he is not Willie Mays or Willie McCovey.

The 1960s and 1970s saw a plethora of great black athletes named Willie, mostly from the South, and it got confusing.

Willie Brown of the Oakland Raiders was never a guy who did much to draw attention away from the game, but in 16 years on the pro battlefields, he most definitely distinguished himself. Davis acquired Brown from the Denver Broncos, where he had already made his mark, tying an NFL/AFL record for interceptions in a game with four versus New York in 1964.

"THE REAL WILLIE BROWN IS SO ENORMOUSLY TALENTED THAT HARDLY ANY QUARTERBACK THINKS IT SPECIALLY CLEVER TO THROW THE BALL NEAR HIM."

—WELLS TWOMBLY

Brown was part of the influx of talent that came to Oakland in 1967, turning a promising franchise into a dominant one that went 13–1, advancing to Super Bowl II against Green Bay.

Brown shares the all-time Raider lead for interceptions with 39 and earned All-Pro honors seven times, in addition to five AFL All-Star appearances and four Pro Bowls. He was named to the All-Time AFL Team in 1969, played in three AFL and six AFC Championship Games, plus Super Bowls II and XI.

Brown's legend was made when, with NFL Films' highlight man John Facenda providing the dramatic voiceover, the camera captured Brown's interception of Fran Tarkenton and his Super Bowl–record 75-yard interception return, clinching the 1977 victory over Minnesota. In slow motion, Brown racehorses down the field, the brilliant Pasadena sunshine providing a backdrop, Raider partisans whoopin' it up. Madden jumps up and down, his wild hair and disheveled shirt flopping around. Dramatic and classical music gives it an operatic quality. The highlights also include Bill King's rat-tat-tat descriptions, which are the essence of broadcast perfection.

Brown also returned interceptions for touchdowns in the playoffs against Miami in 1970 and against Pittsburgh in 1973. He intercepted at least one pass in an NFL-record 16 straight seasons, and had 54 in his brilliant career. This came to a total of 472 return yards and two touchdowns in regular-season play.

Brown played in 205 pro games and was the MVP of the 1965 AFL All-Star Game. He won the 1968 Gorman Award as the "Player Who Best Exemplifies the Pride and Spirit of the Raiders."

He was the defensive captain for 10 years and a selection to the 25-Year AFL-NFL All-Star Team, then picked to enter Canton on his first try in 1984. After football, Brown was a Raider assistant and briefly tried to bring the moribund Long Beach State program back into the fold. He is a member of the Louisiana and Mississippi Sports Halls of Fame, and after Long Beach State, rejoined the Raiders.

"The Real Willie Brown is so enormously talented that hardly any quarterback thinks it specially clever to throw the ball near him," wrote Wells Twombly in *Oakland's Raiders: Fireworks and Fury* in 1973.

Brown was described as a "strong and charming man," a laid-back rural Southerner with a pleasant off-field demeanor. Despite—or, in reality, because of—his interception records, opposing teams often did not throw the ball in his direction, for obvious reasons.

"They don't throw towards me much, it's true," he stated. "But I consider that a rare compliment. I can't relax, though. I fully expect to get the pass on every play, and I stay as close as possible to my man. If I crowd him on the short pass, I may find that he's gone deep. If I play him deep, he'll take the short throw. So I try to stay right on top of him. If I have my man covered, it's going to hold the quarterback up, so our rush line can get him. All this happens in just a few seconds. It always amazes me how long those few seconds seem to take."

Brown came out of Eddie Robinson's program at Grambling before the world had come to fully

BY THE NUMBERS

31—The number of home games Miami had won in a row before losing to the Raiders, 31–21, in the first game of the 1975 season.

TRADING PLACES

There were two main reasons why the Raiders eventually dealt Marcus Allen. First, the drafting of Bo Jackson, who took significant playing time and spotlight from Allen. Then, in 1987 when the players struck, Davis insisted that Allen join a group of veteran stars who crossed the line. Allen refused. After Jackson hurt himself in the January 1991 playoff win against the Bengals, Davis signed free agent Roger Craig. Eventually, Allen joined Joe Montana in Kansas City.

recognize how much talent there was at the little state school in Louisiana. He was a 6′2″, 210-pound tight end, but Robinson ran a ground-oriented offense, so Brown mainly blocked.

The Houston Oilers signed Brown as a free agent and turned him into a defensive back. He learned the position in practice sessions, covering Charley Hennigan (who once caught 101 passes in a single season). The quarterback shredding the secondary was George Blanda. But the Oilers cut Brown. Denver signed him, and he displayed brilliance, but the club was mediocre. Brown was lost in the shuffle, for the most part.

Except, of course, Al Davis had a spy system comparable with the Mossad's. He was scouted, and a full report was provided to Davis, who arranged for a trade that was more like highway robbery. The truth is, Brown's talent was well known in AFL circles, but Denver still let him get away.

"I have come to understand fully now why Lou Saban traded me," said Brown in 1973. "I would have done the same thing if I were the coach. He came into a losing organization. He wanted to bring in his own players—younger players. He did me a favor by trading me to a team like Oakland. He couldn't have been nicer."

Brown's great career is even more impressive when one considers that he was playing man defense during the age of the "bump and run," facing what may have been the most advanced new passing schemes, the best crop of quarterbacks, and the most talented wide receivers the game has ever known.

He was tasked with stopping offenses designed by the likes of Hank Stram, Weeb Ewbank, Sid Gillman, Don Shula, and Chuck Noll. He squared off against quarterbacks the likes of Joe Namath, Len Dawson, John Hadl, Bart Starr, Terry Bradshaw, and Bob Griese, who were throwing to pass-catching talents with names like Don Maynard, Lance Alworth, Otis Taylor, Lynn Swann, John Stallworth, and Paul Warfield.

He gave as good as he got. For the most part, those terrific offensive minds, with those terrific offensive tools at their disposal, chose to throw the ball in the direction of somebody *other than* the Real Willie Brown!

GOLDEN BOY

For the most part, the Raiders have been a team of renegades. Ken Stabler with his hair, his beer, and his broads did not fit the all-American style preferred by Vince Lombardi or Tom Landry.

Fred Biletnikoff was often recalcitrant, bending the rules, speaking his mind.

Jim Plunkett was the poor Mexican-American kid with blind parents, discarded by football until Al Davis picked him off the scrap heap.

As far as some were concerned, Jack Tatum and George Atkinson should have been playing in *The Longest Yard*, not the Coliseum.

Even the great Howie Long, despite his "pretty boy" looks, was a tough street kid from Boston who was unheralded coming out of little Villanova.

Marcus Allen was an exception to the Raider rule. He was a "golden boy"—like Frank Gifford before him, a handsome, charismatic superstar from the University of Southern California. He was the toast of Hollywood

IF ONLY...

Bo Jackson had not been hurt, the baseball/football star from Auburn, who briefly starred for the L.A. Raiders in the late 1980s, probably would have had a Hall of Fame career in one, if not two sports.

who never fit the image of a has-been, overlooked by all who had seen him perform.

Marcus came out of Lincoln High School in San Diego, where he was the team's star quarterback and county Player of the Year, leading his team to the CIF–San Diego title.

"I think they made me quarterback because they felt I was the team leader," said Allen, who also played baseball. "I was no passer of distinction."

The USC coaches switched him to running back when they saw him up close. In his freshman year, he replaced an injured Charles White versus Michigan State and almost broke a touchdown run.

"I'd broken for about 15 yards, and there was one man between me and the goal line," he said. "Then I cut back on the wrong foot, slipped, and I was the loneliest man on that football field."

He played fullback as a sophomore and tailback as a junior.

"He made the switch without a murmur," said John Jackson, an assistant coach of the running game. He broke his nose in a scrimmage but rushed for 649 yards.

"I don't think I ever recovered from that introduction," he said. "My nose has been put back together like a puzzle. But, playing fullback made me more aggressive. However, I was just looking forward to getting back to tailback."

"We recruited Marcus Allen as a defensive back out of San Diego," said coach John Robinson in 1980. "He's 6'3", 195 pounds, and he's terrific. He came to me and said, 'Coach, I want to play tailback. I think I'm the type for the job.' He is, too."

Nicknamed "Young Juice" for his physical resemblance to O.J. Simpson, he employed a similar style in the open field. He was the second leading rusher in the nation as a junior through 10 games but missed the 20–3 win over Notre Dame with an eye injury.

"Marcus has a wide range of skills," said Robinson. "He's an excellent pass receiver along with his running ability. I think he could make it in the NFL as a wide receiver. He's also a fine blocker who picks up blitzes. And he's so durable. When he played fullback, we rarely had to substitute for him."

Marcus Allen (shown being congratulated by Al Davis) was the greatest running back in Raiders history. Allen accumulated 12,243 yards and 123 touchdowns rushing during a 16-year career (11 with the Raiders).

When Allen broke all the national rushing records, earning the 1981 Heisman, combined with his natural charm, he became an iconic figure at Troy.

"That particular time when I won the award, I was very happy because I'd achieved something I wanted to achieve, but I was really happy for my family," said Marcus in *The History of USC Football* DVD. "It was more important for my parents than it was for me, because it was a reflection of all the hard work they'd put in, years ago, all the Pop Warner experiences, my mom being the team mother and my dad being the coach, running back and forth and really giving up their lives for their kids' lives. So for me it was like the first time I had an opportunity to pay back my parents. I remember, my dad is a very loquacious guy, talks non-stop, but for the first time in my lifetime, he was just quiet, and he was speechless. And I know he was nothing but proud, it was *his son*. He could say, 'My son,' and my mom could say, 'My son is known as the best college player in the country.' That's for them, what it's all about, and for me that's what it was all about."

DID YOU KNOW...

That the Raiders all-time record in playoff games is 25–18?

The captain of the 1981 team, Allen set 16 NCAA records and was the first collegian to break 2,000 regular-season yards. He won the Walter Camp and Maxwell trophies, averaging 212.9 yards a game in his senior year. In 1982, the Raiders, in the process of moving from Oakland to L.A., made him their first pick.

Able to continue his football career in the same Coliseum where he had starred in college, Marcus was an instant hit on and off the field. He was the Rookie of the Year and a Pro Bowl running back in 1982. In 1983, he was the best player in the NFL.

The Raiders finished with a 12–4 record behind Marcus's heroics, then beat Joe Theismann and Washington in the Super Bowl. Allen had a spectacular game in the Raiders' 38–9 victory, breaking a long run to put the game away, earning Most Valuable Player honors.

Off the field, Marcus became a Hollywood figure, taken under his wing by the movie star O.J. Simpson. He dated starlets and became a bon vivant, a man about town. It never affected his performance, however. He continued to star for the Raiders year in and year out. The team was upset by the New England Patriots in the 1985 AFC playoffs, however, and took a turn for the worse. In the late 1980s and early 1990s, Raider attendance was down. A dangerous "gang element" permeated the Coliseum, which was a notable contrast to the polished alumni crowds at USC games.

Allen maintained his star status but had a falling out with the irascible Al Davis, who showed no class in dumping Marcus to the Kansas City Chiefs. Now teamed with Joe Montana, who had lost his job in San Francisco to Steve Young and then gone to Kansas City, the two veterans led the Chiefs to their best years since the Mike Garrett Super Bowl teams of the 1960s. Allen retired after the 1997 season. He is an inductee in the USC, College, and Pro Football Halls of Fame. Like many other Trojans, Marcus was media savvy and put it to good use as a TV commentator.

In 1994, when O.J.'s wife was murdered, Marcus found himself caught in the vortex of publicity and tabloid journalism surrounding the case. A persistent rumor made its way to the papers that Marcus had been seeing Nicole Simpson, thus enraging O.J. Allen was able to distance himself from the rumor and O.J. while holding on to his status as a class act.

HOWIE, STORK, RAIDERETTES, AND THE "FIVE-OH"

Naturally, since the Raiders are one of the all-time great pro football franchises, they have produced all-time great players. These men have been have been recognized with induction into the Pro Football Hall of Fame in Canton, Ohio.

Howie Long was a defensive end who joined the *Oakland* Raiders with their second pick of the 1981 Draft, after having earned the MVP award in the Blue-Gray game his senior year at little Villanova. In his 13 years, he was associated with the team in Los Angeles. Howie was born for Hollywood. He married a USC Law School graduate and, with his all-American image, became a poster boy for the team, which in the 1980s was glamorized in a way they never were in Oakland.

The Raiderette cheerleaders, who were not considered to be in the same league as their Dallas Cowboys counterparts during the Oakland years, suddenly became one of the hottest dance groups

Bo Jackson was one of the greatest talents in football history, but injuries and the fact that he was also playing professional baseball limited him to a part-time, four-year career with the Raiders. When playing, he rushed for more than 2,700 yards and 16 touchdowns.

in pro sports. The talent pool of aspiring models, actresses, and dancers who tried out for the Raiderettes, in an effort to promote their careers, was much greater than in other cities.

In L.A., the Raiders and their fans descended upon a restaurant/bar called the California Pizza and Pasta Company on Sundays after home games. Also known as the "502 Club," it was a sports bar located across the street from USC, thus it was within walking distance of the Coliseum. A longtime hangout of USC athletes, the "Five-Oh" was the happening place to be, with Raiderettes and Raiders partying together with 'SC players and average fans. The NFL has strict rules about player-cheerleader fraternization, but if these rules were in place then, they were not enforced.

Most of the players and the Raiderettes lived in the South Bay (the team trained in El Segundo), so it was common for everybody to start out at the "Five-Oh" and, after dinner and drinks, caravan to Redondo's Red Onion or some other dance club.

Howie had a "rock star" image with the fans, especially the ladies, but he was not known as a wild party guy. He had worked too hard to get where he was and had the gift of stability. He usually was not part of the team's "floating cocktail party." On July 29, 2000, his stability was rewarded with induction into Canton.

He played his entire career for the Raiders, making a record-tying eight Pro Bowl appearances in his career. Long moved into the starting role with the Raiders beginning in the fifth game of the strike-shortened 1982 season. He became just the second Raider defensive lineman to make a Pro Bowl and earned first- or second-team All-Pro in 1983, 1984, 1985, 1986, 1989, and 1990. He also was named All-AFC four times.

DID YOU KNOW...

That, aside from John Madden and Howie Long, several other Raiders have been involved in radio and TV broadcasting work over the years? They include game analysts Tom Flores and Jim Plunkett, George Atkinson (who has hosted a call-in show), Marcus Allen, Ronnie Lott, and Eric Dickerson.

TOP 10

The Raiders were notorious for wild parties at their Santa Rosa training camp. The following are the top 10 most notorious "campers":

1. John Matuszak
2. Ken Stabler
3. Lyle Alzado
4. Ben Davidson
5. George Atkinson
6. Jack Tatum
7. Fred Biletnikoff
8. Tom Keating
9. Dave Casper
10. Ted Hendricks

In 1985, Long accounted for 10 sacks, with at least one in eight games. He was selected as the Raider Lineman's Club Defensive Lineman of the Year by his teammates. Although he missed much of the 1988 season due to injury, he still managed to record three sacks and intercept the first pass of his career, which he returned 73 yards in a game against the Houston Oilers.

He is a member of the NFL's All-Decade team of the 1980s, recorded 84 career sacks, not including 7.5 sacks in 1981 before the sack was an official NFL statistic. Howie parlayed his popularity and intelligence into a long career as an NFL TV analyst and commercial spokesman. One of his teammates on the great Raider defenses of the 1980s was linebacker Ted Hendricks, who was inducted into the Pro Football Hall of Fame on August 4, 1990.

Hendricks, known as the "Mad Stork" because he was tall and ran the field with his arms flapping like a stork, played 15 years in the NFL. He joined Oakland in a trade with Green Bay in 1975. He was with the Silver and Black for nine years and played in 131 consecutive league games with the Raiders, 215 in his career, the most by any linebacker in NFL history.

Ted was a member of all three Raider "World Champions of Professional Football" (1976, 1980, and 1983). He intercepted 26 passes for 332 yards and one touchdown while recovering 16 opponents' fumbles, and shares the NFL record for most safeties in a pro career with four. He also shares the postseason NFL record for most opponents fumbles recovered in a career with four. He scored three touchdowns in his career on a fumble recovery, an interception return, and the return of a blocked punt.

Hendricks was named All-AFC seven times, All-NFC once, and played in eight AFC-NFC Pro Bowls. He was originally a second-round pick in the 1969 Draft by Baltimore, where he was a member of Baltimore's Super Bowl V championship team. He played for the Colts before being traded to Green Bay in 1974. Henricks was named to the NFL 75th Anniversary All-Time Team in 1994.

At the University of Miami, he was a three-time All-American linebacker/defensive end, named to some All-America teams as a sophomore in 1966, and was a consensus All-America choice in 1967 and 1968. The 6′7″, 220-pounder was named college Lineman of the Year by United Press International as a senior.

Hendricks was moved to outside linebacker when he joined the Colts. He distinguished himself as a pass rusher and kick blocker.

When the new World Football League was organized in 1974, its teams signed a number of players to future contracts to begin playing after their NFL contracts expired. Hendricks was among them. When the announcement was made, the Colts traded him to the Green Bay Packers for the 1974 season. Because of the WFL's financial problems, Hendricks never played in the league. Instead, Al Davis obtained his rights from the Packers and signed him.

RONNIE LOTT

No, Ronnie Lott is not remembered as a Raider. He was only an L.A. Raider for two years (1990–1991) and not part of any glorious Raider Super Bowl teams. But Lott is considered one of the greatest football players of all time. He cast such a giant shadow over the game that his short Raider tenure is one that is looked upon with great pride.

Lott was the captain of the USC Trojans, where he earned All-America honors. Lott may well be the noblest Trojan of them all. The son of a military officer, raised with discipline, respect for authority, and poise, he starred at the appropriately named Eisenhower High School in Rialto, east of Los Angeles. At that time, the community, which revolved around oil derricks, produced extraordinarily tough kids and great prep teams, giving the town enormous pride. He played on USC's 1978 national champions and the 1979 Rose Bowl champs. A member of the College Hall of Fame and the team's 1980 MVP, Lott also won the Davis-Teschke Award as the most inspirational Trojan. He was a chip off the Marv Goux block—the very epitome of football toughness, pride, intelligence, and fierce loyalty. Lott is said by some to be the hardest hitter of all time. Who can say? Those who got hit by him. They are the ones who said it.

Lott was the eighth pick of the 1981 Draft. Safety Kenny Easley of UCLA was actually considered the better prospect, chosen ahead of him by Seattle. Easley was a fine pro, but Lott is the stuff legends are made of. In an interview with Bill Walsh in 2001, this author asked whether he would have chosen Easley over Lott had the Seahawks not picked him. Walsh denied that he would have, despite rumors that at the time he subscribed to Easley's scouting reports. He also adamantly denied that he had considered his own Stanford quarterback, Steve Dils, over Joe Montana during the 1979 Draft. Whether Walsh's memory was faulty or just convenient, fate or good judgment led him to make all the right moves. Montana and Lott, opponents in the 1978 "battle of L.A.," were the cornerstones of the greatest dynasty in professional football history. The 49ers won five Super Bowl titles between the 1981 and 1994 seasons.

> **IF ONLY...**
>
> Ronnie Lott had been drafted by the Raiders instead of San Francisco in 1981, he and his USC teammate, Marcus Allen, might have developed the greatest of all Raider dynasties at the L.A. Coliseum in the 1980s.

While Montana had already been San Francisco's quarterback on losing teams in 1979 and '80, Lott's arrival made them an instant winner of their first Super Bowl. On a team that also included Charle "Tree" Young, the 49ers beat Anthony Munoz and the Bengals. The 1984 49ers are thought by some to be the best pro team ever, or at least the best offensively. Lott and

Montana starred on repeat world champions from 1988 to 1989.

In 1991, Lott returned to the Coliseum when he signed with the Los Angeles Raiders. He inspired that team to success through sheer inspiration and hard hitting in his two years there, before finishing up with the Jets.

Lott was a perfect Raider. Had Oakland drafted him in 1981 instead of San Francisco, the next decade might have been much different. The terms "commitment to excellence" and "pride and poise" perfectly embodied Lott's work ethic and on-field willingness to hit with the force of a jackhammer. He was not the biggest, the fastest, or the strongest. On the surface, others seemed tougher than the quiet, reserved Lott, but none were so willing to lay their bodies on the line. Lott called his autobiography *Total Impact.*

"Right before impact, my adrenaline rises," he wrote. "I can actually feel it surge. I can taste it. An inner force tells me to push harder. Something deep inside says, 'Let everything go into this hit. Bring it from your toes!'"

Lott is, of course, in the USC Hall of Fame, the College Hall of Fame, and the Pro Football Hall of Fame in Canton, Ohio. Like so many articulate Trojans, the ruggedly handsome Lott worked for a while as a TV football commentator. He remains committed to his alma mater, and his two years as a Raider were good ones.

THE KING OF THEM ALL

The man was an artist. The da Vinci, Michelangelo, or Frank Lloyd Wright of broadcasting.

Bill King was the long-time announcer for the Oakland A's, and before that the voice of the Raiders, Warriors, Giants, and California Golden Bears. He had one of the most recognizable deliveries in sport. The goateed Sausalito resident was a highly recognizable Bay Area figure who was even stopped and asked if he was the devil.

The man was a talkative angel.

"I always liked to talk," said the Bloomington, Illinois, native of how he got his start in broadcasting with the Armed Forces

TOP 10

All-Time Sports Announcers

1. Vin Scully
2. **Bill King**
3. Keith Jackson
4. Dick Enberg
5. Chick Hearn
6. Ernie Harwell
7. Jack Buck
8. Red Barber
9. **John Madden**
10. Pat Summerall

Radio Network, while stationed in the Marianas Islands after World War II, during a 2001 Coliseum interview.

"It was great duty. I guess you could say I was the 'Robin Williams of Guam,'" said King, referring to Williams's role as Adrian Cronauer in *Good Morning, Vietnam* (1987).

Like so many veterans, King migrated to California and was the right man in the right spot when the Giants brought major league baseball to San Francisco.

"I worked with Russ Hodges and Lon Simmons on Giants games on KSFO," recalled King, as well as Cal games, then the Raiders and Golden State Warriors.

"Football by far is the hardest sport to do," he said. "Basketball is the easiest. In baseball, you have to be careful when you open your mouth not to show how stupid you are."

King announced California football as well as the 1959 Bears' national championship basketball team, coached by the legendary Pete Newell.

King achieved his most lasting fame announcing the most dramatic moments of the most exciting team in pro football history, the Al Davis Oakland Raiders of the 1960s, '70s, and '80s. He followed the team to Los Angeles from 1982 to 1994, but left in a dispute with Davis when the team returned to Oakland in 1995.

"Davis is a fascinating man," King said of the mysterious Raiders owner. "He coached and was commissioner of the AFL."

Was Davis the "genius" behind the wide-open passing game of the old American Football League?

"Sid Gillman was the real force of the new offensive philosophy of the AFL," exclaimed King of the former San Diego Chargers coach, "but Al absorbed those philosophies. Interestingly, though, nobody won with over 40 passes in those days."

In 1970, backup quarterback George Blanda passed and kicked

the team to a series of miraculous wins, and King's legend was made when he said, "George Blanda is *king of the world!*" after he kicked a long field goal to beat Cleveland. His "Wells to the right, Biletnikoff slot left" was a trademark, too, but two phrases define King's football broadcasts.

One stems from the 1974 AFC playoff win over Miami, when he stated that the Raiders were only yards from "the Promised Land" just before Clarence Davis's touchdown grab gave them victory.

The other is "Holy Toledo," which King used mostly to described touchdowns. "It's better than saying, 'Holy s**t,'" was King's explanation.

"Ken Stabler was a delight," King said of Snake. "He's the only athlete I've ever known who had no fear of failure. He's the converse of Dennis Eckersley, who, like most athletes, drove himself through fear of failure.

"The Raiders' party scene was over-hyped, but I will say that their rowdiness at the El Rancho Tropicana in Santa Rosa lived up to the legend. John Madden was fairly true to the image of him, but he was totally absorbed in his job. Now, he truly loves what he does because he's glad not to have to have the tunnel vision required of a head coach."

King was a literate man who made references to the likes of Aristotle and Fitzgerald, among others, but he "cannot explain what comes out of my mouth."

King saw all the great ones.

"Rick Barry is intelligent and has a huge ego," King said, "but I'm always sorry when I hear him say some of the disparaging things that get him in trouble."

King supported Ray Guy as a football Hall of Famer, but was not sure of Stabler's qualifications.

One thing was for sure. King has Hall of Fame credentials in at least two sports. Shortly after the 2005 baseball season ended, King went in for minor surgery but died of complications on the operating table. He had planned to return to the A's in 2006 and probably beyond.

Bay Area radio stations honored his memory with tributes, stories, and classic broadcasts for a week after his passing. For those who did not grow up with him, or had not heard his Oakland Raider and Golden State Warrior work, it was a revelation.

King was a local Bay Area radio announcer. He was never a national figure or TV personality (like Madden), aside from games that may have been carried nationwide or the classic highlights on ESPN or NFL Films. He toiled in Oakland, part of a large enough market, but not New York or Chicago. When he worked Los Angeles Raider games in the 1980s and '90s, it opened his reputation up to a huge, new audience. A decade after the team's departure, any knowledgeable Los Angeleno includes King among the town's all-time greatest sports announcers.

While the likes of Vin Scully, Dick Enberg, Bob Costas, and Keith Jackson are revered national figures, those who are intimately familiar with King's work unhesitatingly list him among the very, very best sports announcers of all times. He was considered a fine baseball announcer, but that was his third-best sport. Whether King or Chick Hearn is the best basketball announcer ever is debatable. Each had his own traits, but King's sharp eye for detail on the hardcourt was unparalleled. Hearn had more tricks and phrases. King was just a whirling dervish of perfectly delivered syntax, seemingly describing what was going through the player's *minds*, in addition to their physical skills.

TRIVIA

What did Bill King say about Ken Stabler when, in the second half of the Raiders' Super Bowl win over the Vikings, it was obvious the game was won?

Find the answers on page 177.

But King's football broadcasts remain works of art. *Nobody* was ever a better radio football voice. Nobody. Keith Jackson's TV persona was unique, but King on the radio was *numero uno.* Any poll of Raider fans from the 1970s reveals that sentiment. The team was so great, so exciting, that of course he was given fabulous material. But in the mind's eye, the "greatness that is the Raiders" was as much in the telling—by Bill King—as in the incredible deeds of the players themselves.

He will be missed.

A LITTLE INTRIGUE

FOOTBALL'S CIA

By the late 1960s, Al Davis and his Raiders had a well-earned reputation as the most secretive organization in professional sports. Over the years, as organization men have retired, trades occurred, and free agency and other factors played out, slowly but surely some of the team's trade secrets became known. Nevertheless, they remain football's version of the Central Intelligence Agency.

But few have ever really known what went on behind closed doors. Many players do not know certain things, as the methods are compartmentalized on a "need to know basis," just like at Langley. Reporters have never been given free access to practices or meetings.

In the early 1970s, the Raider media guide listed only one scout, Ken Herock. The rest operated in secret, theoretically telling their wives and children they sold insurance while covertly evaluating collegiate football prospects, castoffs, and semipros.

"Where to this week, honey?"

"Uh, Norman, Oklahoma."

"And next week?"

"Lincoln, Nebraska. Big seminar on annuities, dear."

For years, Davis entrusted much of the organizational work to Don McMahon. McMahon pitched for the San Francisco Giants. He went to high school with Davis in Brooklyn. Apparently, Davis needed to know somebody since boyhood in order to feel safe

BY THE NUMBERS

15—Division championships won by the Raiders (1967–1970, 1972–1976, 1983, 1985, 1990, 2000–2002).

with him, not unlike Mafia culture, which he has studied and made use of in his own organizational structure.

McMahon reportedly headed a shadowy group of "gophers" whose job it was to "burrow under the surface," scouting collegians and also-ran professionals—players cut by NFL squads or languishing in Canada, who might have a year or two left in the tank for a cheap price.

Ron Wolf was the Raiders' director of player personnel, and while Davis loomed large over the organization, Wolf is considered one of the great genius figures of the professional scene. In Oakland, he effectuated the Davis mystique, wearing glasses that made him look like "twin television sets," according to San Francisco *Examiner* writer Wells Twombly.

Like Davis, Wolf's "playing career" was nebulous at best. Nobody quite knew whether Wolf played at Maryville College in Tennessee or the University of Oklahoma. In many ways, Davis's organization was the model for Billy Beane's *Moneyball* style, which built the Oakland A's baseball team into a powerhouse in the 2000s. In this regard, an executive's experience on the field of play was not considered important. Rather, his knowledge, gleaned from unorthodox sources, could be used to create better football success.

Davis studied politics, history, the Mafia, and warfare, using techniques first detailed in Sun-Tzu's *The Art of War* to build his organization and acquire players other executives passed on or did not know about. Beane became the same kind of man, reading historical biographies, then using techniques picked up from those readings to develop great teams on a budget. He hired young men from Ivy League schools with little traditional baseball background but who were bright, well read, and thought like he did. His methods have been very successful.

Al Davis is one of the most colorful characters in pro football history. The president and the managing general partner of the Raiders, he has always done things his own way, including relocating the team twice—moving first to Los Angeles, then back to Oakland.

Wolf's greatest attribute was a photographic memory, which he is alleged to have put to use for the U.S. government prior to his work with the Raiders. In the early 1970s, the Raider media guide said the following about him: "Wolf was an intelligence specialist in West Berlin prior to joining the Raiders."

It was Wolf who presided over a series of drafts in which the Raiders chose players from small schools and traditional black colleges—players who went on to All-Pro careers while All-Americans from traditional powers failed. Players like linebacker Phil Villapiano, wide receiver Mike Siani, fullback Marv Hubbard, and linebacker Gerald Irons were low-profile guys who contributed to the "greatness that is the Raiders."

Ben Davidson was a great big kid from Los Angeles, turned down by four teams before Wolf picked him up and the organization developed him into one of the game's fiercest defensive ends.

"What we try to do is find 'Raider-types' and adapt them to our system, rather than look for players of divergent skills and try to find a system that fits them all," Davis said.

Davis became obsessed with the waiver lists, which was how he acquired George Blanda after Houston released him at age 39.

"George helped us win a lot of important games, and he became a folk hero in the bargain," said Davis. "It has been a satisfactory arrangement for both parties."

In 1973, the Raiders chose a punter, Ray Guy from Southern Mississippi. Few teams "waste" their first pick on a punter, but Guy turned out to be one of the greatest, if not *the* greatest, punters in NFL history, as well as one of the finest athletes Oakland ever produced. He is not in the Hall of Fame, but he should be and eventually will be.

That Jon Gruden was 34 years old when he was hired by the Raiders?

Otis Sistrunk never went to college. An odd character, he fit right in with the Raiders, who joked that his alma mater was "the University of Mars." He was a castoff of the Rams, who unloaded him on Davis. Davis already knew everything about Sistrunk, and that he did not fit into the Rams' salary structure. He became an integral part of Raider championship teams.

Raider practices have always been closed. They have never gone out of their way to accommodate writers. For this, Davis has found he has enemies in the media. He has never cared. His fan base has always identified with this "outsider" status. They are the hard hats, the militants, and the recalcitrants of Oakland, Hayward, San Leandro, San Lorenzo—roughnecks who disdain the effete ways of San Francisco and root for the "shot and a beer" team that has called the Oakland Coliseum home for so many years.

The team has always found a home for players who display these traits. Ken Stabler, considered a "wild child," suspended by Alabama football coach Bear Bryant for aberrant behavior—his long hair, lascivious lifestyle, and love of wild partying symbolized this.

Davidson was one of the first to ever wear a handlebar moustache, long before Rollie Fingers and the A's stylized the look in the 1970s. He was viewed as a dangerous giant, but any Davids playing for the Chiefs, Jets, or Chargers never felled this Goliath.

Gene Upshaw, Art Shell, and Bob Brown were black players with chips on their shoulders, but when they got to Oakland they realized Davis did not see color. Given the free and unfettered opportunity to demonstrate their abilities, they took full advantage of the situation, forging legendary careers.

THE RAIDERS PLUNDER THE 'NINERS

By 2001, they were baaaaaack! The Raiders were living up to their reputation for plundering the local citizenry like Mediterranean pirates. The hottest topic in the Bay Area was one that created drawn lines and had everyone picking a side. Was Al Davis going to ride into San Francisco, kidnap the icon Jerry Rice from under the nose of the wine drinkers, and haul him like captured booty back to O-town?

This scribe, then the lead sports columnist for *The* (San Francisco) *Examiner,* had it on good authority that the Raiders would sign Rice. There were issues to be worked out, but in the end, Davis gets what Davis wants. The 1980 Raiders made the Super Bowl on the strength of veterans, and that was the logical push for them to make.

This was like seeing the barbarians come in and have their way with your women. The Raiders getting Rice was like the A's

The Raiders made waves in the Bay Area in 2001 when they lured legendary wide receiver Jerry Rice (shown in the Oakland offensive huddle) away from the rival 49ers. Rice had two strong seasons with the Raiders, leading the team to a spot in Super Bowl XXXVII.

getting Willie Mays to switch addresses back in 1970. If you were a 49er fan, how did this make you feel?

Before the deal was made, it was opinion time for the "49er Faithful" and "the Black Hole" fans, because the choice was Rice, Andre Rison, or neither one?

Rison or Rice? Oh, man, are you kidding? These were a couple of guys who were so fast in their prime that they could turn the switch off and be under the sheets before the lights went out.

Davis, Jon Gruden, and the Raiders faced a public conundrum. Which one did they want? Did they want either one playing alongside Tim Brown? Rice was not technically available, but Bill Walsh, in fact, listed one of his greatest final accomplishments his handling of Rice's *departure* from the 49ers. Free agent Rison could be had.

At the time, Oakland was there, brother. One game away from the Big Dance in 2000. Quarterback Rich Gannon was no spring chicken, but he had some bullets left in his arsenal.

Leases and lawsuits will not prevent a return to L.A. (I refer ye to the archives of history.) The Raiders then and now need to draw sell-outs and light up the Bay Area TV market. Rice would put butts in the seats. Plus, this was about winning that year.

There is no substitute.

Rice was not the deep threat he had been, but he could still make important plays and be a fabulous weapon for Gannon, who was an outstanding scrambler and would give Rice time to juke defenders. Thirty-nine or no 39 (his age in October 2001), if you gave Rice time to juke defenders, explosive things happened.

The Raiders also had to decide whether their schematic was to beat Baltimore in the AFC title game, or to best set themselves up for Western Division opponents. Walsh set up his offense to beat the 4–3, and San Francisco ran rampant over Denver in the 1990 Super Bowl. Gannon lobbied for Rison in 2000 because of their Kansas City connection, and the move paid off handsomely when Rison took James Jett's place and scored the winning touchdown in the opener against San Diego, despite not knowing the playbook. Most of the Raider players liked Rison, who resurrected his career there. In 2001, he wanted to re-sign with his 2000 team.

But Rice would give them more weapons against 2000 world champion Baltimore, who had stifled Oakland in the AFC title game. For that reason, it was logical to get Rice. Rice could cover the middle and go deep. In May of 2001, this scribe ventured over to the Coliseum to cover an A's game when the "Rice or Rison?" question was hanging in the air. I cornered A's announcer Greg Papa, also the Raiders' radio man, and put the question to him.

Rison has "done a lot of living, if you know what I mean," Papa told me, but asked to be quoted as a "Raiders source," which he still is, a high-ranking one. "For this reason among others, Rice brings more to the table."

Papa plainly informed me that he had the inside scoop on the decision and that "it's gonna be Rice." I told him I was going to press with this and needed to know for sure, and he thus assured me. Knowing what I know, Papa must have had Davis's authority to speak so plainly, albeit anonymously.

I wrote a column for *The Examiner* arguing that Tim Brown was a possession receiver, but Rice could cover the middle and still go deep on occasion, that he was indeed the best choice, and in fact *was* the choice. I broke the story. An assistant editor at *The Examiner* tried to tell me that "Papa's not a source. He's a member of the media like you and me."

Papa was *not* a member of the media like we were. No announcer of the Oakland Raiders ever will be so long as Al Davis is their owner. He was an *employee* of Davis, serving entirely at the pleasure of the Man in Black. Calling him a member of the media, at least in the context of his association with Davis and the Raiders, was like calling the White House press secretary a member of the White House press corps. Bill King could detail what happens when the team's announcer has a disagreement with the team's owner. He is not an independent journalist "covering" the Raiders. So, no matter what that editor said back in '01, Greg Papa was highly, precisely, and to quintessential effect, a *high-ranking Raiders source!*

I wrote that James Jett offered enough speed to keep the defense honest, although Gannon could not consistently get the ball downfield. If Jett would show that he could catch the ball, though, the Raiders would have more weapons than the Army. This strengthened the Rice choice. On the best rushing team in the AFC from 2000, opponents not only would have to defend in reality, but make extra preparations.

Meanwhile, Gannon, Tyrone Wheatley, and the rest of the team would find holes widen for them. Brown and Rice could be the best twosome in the league, I opined.

Rison's agent was lobbying to get his guy a deal, but Oakland, I said, should wait for—and indeed had already decided on—Rice.

The question was whether Rice and Brown would find that Oakland "was not too big a town for both to hold one end of the Lombardi Trophy."

A week or so later, my breaking story was proven right as rain, just as my *source,* Greg Papa, had told me it would. As I predicted, Rice and Brown became a dynamic pass-catching duo working with Gannon, and came within one win—and maybe Barret Robbins's bipolar night in Tijuana—from both holding "one end of the Lombardi Trophy."

DID YOU KNOW...

That Rich Gannon was the MVP of the 2001 and 2002 Pro Bowls?

Greg Papa continues to be a Raider source. Had he spoken out of school that 2001 afternoon, he would no longer be. That assistant editor? The last I heard he was working for a free paper that nobody ever read, until it went out of business.

ALL-TIME RAIDERS TEAM

DEFENSE

Position	Starter (honorable mention in parentheses)
DE	Howie Long (Chester McGlockton)
DE	Ben Davidson (Greg Townsend)
DT	Tom Keating
DT	John Matuszak (Otis Sistrunk)
OLB	Ted Hendricks
OLB	Rod Martin (Phil Villapiano)
ML	Dan Conners (Matt Millen, Greg Biekert)
CB	Willie Brown
CB	Mike Haynes (Lester Hayes)
SS	Mike Davis (George Atkinson)
FS	Jack Tatum (Vann McElroy)

OFFENSE

Position	Starter (honorable mention in parentheses)
LT	Art Shell
LG	Gene Upshaw
C	Jim Otto (Don Mosebar, Dave Dalby)

Hard-partying defensive lineman John Matuszak was a stalwart on Oakland's Super Bowl XI and XV teams before moving on to an acting career. His self-professed heavy drug use likely contributed to his death at the age of 38 from heart failure.

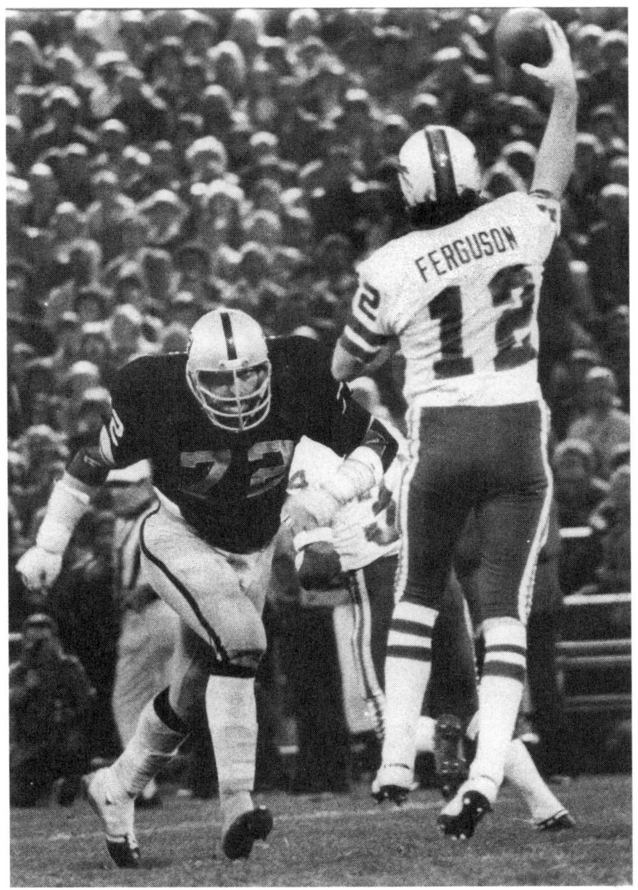

RT	John Vella (Harry Schuh, Henry Lawrence)
RG	George Buehler (Steve Wisniewski, Mickey Marvin)
TE	Dave Casper (Todd Christensen, Raymond Chester, Billy Cannon)
WR	Fred Biletnikoff (Warren Wells, Art Powell)
WR	Tim Brown (Cliff Branch)
HB	Marcus Allen (Clarence Davis)
FB	Mark van Eeghen (Marv Hubbard, Frank Hawkins)
QB	Ken Stabler (Jim Plunkett, Daryle Lamonica, Rich Gannon, Tom Flores)

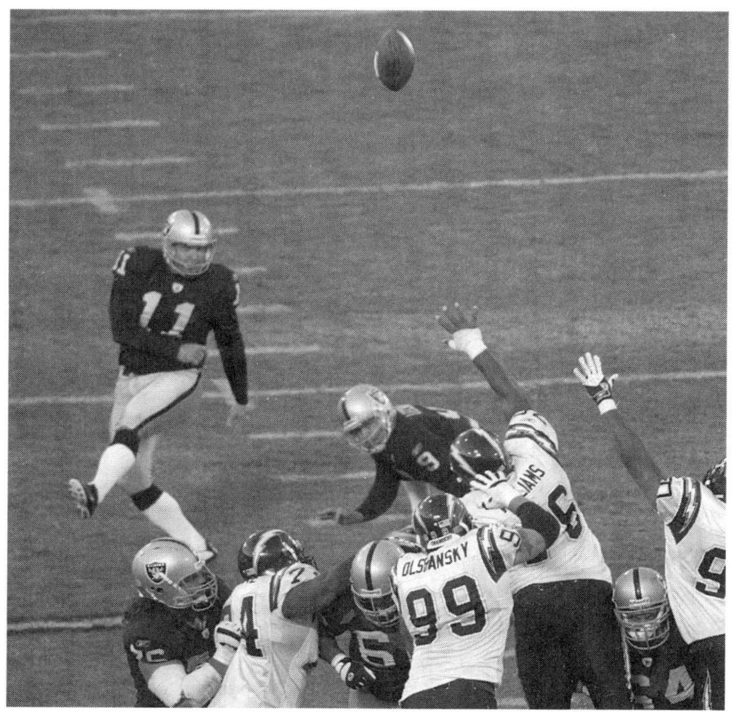

Despite being hampered by legal problems off the field, Sebastian Janikowski has been a success on the field. The Polish-born kicker with the booming leg connected on nearly 77 percent of the field goals he attempted in his first eight seasons with the Raiders.

SPECIAL TEAMS

Position	Starter (honorable mention in parentheses)
KR	George Atkinson
PR	George Atkinson (Tim Brown)
PK	George Blanda
P	Ray Guy
C	John Madden (Tom Flores)

TRIVIA ANSWERS

Page 8: Frank Youell was an East Bay undertaker.

Page 11: Five Raiders have been voted league Player of the Year or MVP. Quarterback Daryle Lamonica was named AFL Player of the Year in 1967 and 1969. Quarterback Ken Stabler (1974), running back Marcus Allen (1985), and quarterback Rich Gannon (2002) were named NFL MVPs.

Page 75: Prior to the start of the 1976 season, Al Davis gained sole control of the franchise when Wayne Valley sold all of his shares.

Page 82: George Blanda played pro football for 26 years (1949–1958, 1960–1975).

Page 109: The Raiders scored 468 points in 1967, holding opponents to a mere 233.

Page 119: Defensive back Skip Thomas dubbed himself "Dr. Death."

Page 127: Three Raiders have been named Super Bowl MVP: wide receiver Fred Biletnikoff (Super Bowl XI), quarterback Jim Plunkett (Super Bowl XV), and running back Marcus Allen (Super Bowl XVIII).

Page 131: Six Heisman Trophy winners have played for the Raiders. They include LSU's Billy Cannon (1959), Stanford's Jim Plunkett (1970), USC's Marcus Allen (1981), Auburn's Bo Jackson (1985), Notre Dame's Tim Brown (1987), and Michigan's Charles Woodson (1997).

Page 164: Toward the end of Super Bowl XI, Bill King said, "Jascha Heifetz never played a violin with more dexterity than Kenny Stabler is playing the Minnesota Vikings defense this afternoon at the Rose Bowl stadium in Pasadena."

SOURCES

Allen, Marcus and Carlton Stowers. *The Autobiography of Marcus Allen*. New York: St. Martin's Press, 1997.

Dickey, Glenn. *Just Win, Baby: Al Davis and His Raiders*. New York: Harcourt, 1991.

LaMarre, Tom. *Stadium Stories: Oakland Raiders*. Globe Pequot, 2003.

Lott, Ronnie. *Total Impact*. New York: Doubleday, 1991.

Otto, Jim. *Otto: The Pain of Glory*. Champaign, IL: Sagamore Publishing, 2000.

Plunkett, Jim and Dave Newhouse. *The Jim Plunkett Story*. New York: Dell Publishing Co., 1982.

Ribowsly, Mark. *Slick: The Silver-and-Black Life of Al Davis*. New York: Macmillan Publishing Co., 1991.

Simmons, Ira. *Black Knight: Al Davis and His Raiders*. Prima, 1990.

Travers, Steven. "A King Walks Amongst Us." *The* (San Francisco) *Examiner*. May 18, 2001.

Travers, Steven. "Raiders Will Plunder Niners Again." *The* (San Francisco) *Examiner*. May 15, 2001.

Travers, Steven. *One Night, Two Teams: Alabama vs. USC and the Game That Changed a Nation*. Lanham, MD: Taylor Trade Publishing, 2007.

Twombly, Wells. *Blanda: Alive and Kicking.* Nash Publications, 1972.

Twombly, Wells. *Oakland's Raiders: Fireworks and Fury.* New York: Prentice-Hall, 1973.